INFLUENCER MARKETING BEYOND THE HYPE

BUILDING AUTHENTIC PARTNERSHIPS FOR LASTING IMPACT

CARLY-JENNINGS BROWN

TABLE OF CONTENTS

Introduction: Why Authentic Influencer Marketing
Matters   1
Chapter 1: The Modern Influencer Landscape   4
Chapter 2: Defining Authenticity in Partnerships   14
Chapter 3: Aligning Brand Values and Influencer
Persona   25
Chapter 4: Identifying the Right Influencers   35
Chapter 5: Building Relationships with Influencers 48
Chapter 6: Creating Compelling, Collaborative
Content   62
Chapter 7: Nurturing Long-Term Partnerships   76
Chapter 8: Measuring Success Beyond Likes and
Shares   90
Chapter 9: Emerging Trends in Authentic Influencer
Marketing   103
Chapter 10: Preparing for the Future of Influencer
Marketing   116
Chapter 11: Future-Proofing Your Brand's Influencer
Marketing Strategy   129
Chapter 12: Evaluating and Optimizing Your
Influencer Marketing Strategy   142
Conclusion: The Power of Authentic Influence   156
Appendices: Essential Resources, Tools, and
Communities for Influencer Marketing Success   158
Final Thoughts   165

Introduction: Why Authentic Influencer Marketing Matters

Influencer marketing has transformed the way brands reach consumers, evolving from a niche tactic into a multi-billion-dollar industry that is shaping the future of digital marketing. What once started as a strategy to leverage the popularity of social media personalities has become an essential approach for brands seeking to build deeper, more meaningful relationships with their audiences. However, as influencer marketing has grown, so has the demand for authenticity. Consumers today are savvy; they can quickly spot insincerity, and they seek genuine connections over hollow endorsements.

This book is a guide to navigating the complexities of this landscape, helping brands move beyond superficial influencer strategies to create partnerships that are rooted in trust, relevance, and shared values. Authentic influencer marketing isn't about vanity metrics or quick gains; it's about cultivating relationships that build long-term loyalty, foster trust, and connect with audiences on a personal level.

Why is authenticity so critical in influencer marketing? The answer lies in consumer behavior. Studies show that people today want to buy from brands that align with their values, respect their intelligence, and communicate honestly. Influencers play a unique role in this environment—they are trusted voices, often seen as friends or relatable figures who share glimpses of their lives and experiences. When influencers genuinely advocate for a brand, their followers take notice. But when partnerships feel forced or transactional, the message falls flat, eroding both the influencer's and the brand's credibility.

In the chapters that follow, this book will take you step-by-step through the process of creating authentic, impactful influencer partnerships. From understanding your brand's core values and identifying influencers who align with them, to fostering long-term relationships and measuring success beyond likes and shares, this guide offers a comprehensive roadmap for brands seeking to build sustainable, meaningful influence.

You'll learn how to create campaigns that resonate, establish mutually beneficial relationships with influencers, and develop a strategy that adapts to the evolving landscape of digital marketing. Along the way, we'll explore emerging trends, ethical considerations, and the latest tools and metrics that can help brands track real impact.

Ultimately, **"Influencer Marketing Beyond the Hype"** is about moving beyond the transactional, toward a marketing approach that puts people and values at the forefront. By embracing authenticity, brands can not only grow their reach but also create loyal, engaged communities around their products and services. This book is here to guide you on that journey, helping you leverage the true power of authentic influence in a way that resonates, builds trust, and leaves a lasting impact.

Chapter 1: The Modern Influencer Landscape

Introduction

The world of influencer marketing has exploded in recent years, becoming one of the most impactful ways for brands to connect with audiences in a digital-first age. Traditional ads, while still relevant, often lack the personal touch that modern consumers crave. Instead, people turn to trusted figures online—those who share relatable stories, offer valuable insights, and maintain authentic connections with their followers. These are the influencers. While influencers range widely in their reach and areas of focus, each has the potential to shape opinions, inspire actions, and foster trust in ways few other marketing channels can.

To succeed in influencer marketing, brands need to understand who they're working with. Gone are the days when celebrity endorsements were enough. The influencer landscape has expanded to include figures who may not be household names but still command attention within their specific niches. This chapter dives into the different types of influencers, the role social media platforms play in influencer marketing, and the importance of trust in building meaningful, lasting partnerships.

Section 1: The Types of Influencers

In today's digital environment, influencers come in all shapes and sizes. From the millions of followers of a mega influencer to the small but fiercely loyal audience of a nano influencer, each category offers unique strengths. Here's a breakdown of the types of influencers brands encounter:

1. Mega Influencers

Mega influencers typically have over a million followers and are often celebrities outside of social media—actors, musicians, athletes, and public figures who have leveraged their fame to amass large followings. Their reach is enormous, and partnering with them can guarantee a certain level of visibility. However, mega influencers' impact is often limited in niche areas, as followers may be more interested in their celebrity status than their opinions on specific products.

Brands with substantial budgets aiming for broad visibility may consider mega influencers, but they must be aware of the potential for these endorsements to feel impersonal. For example, a famous pop star endorsing a new fashion line may create a lot of buzz, but followers may question the authenticity of the endorsement, assuming it's driven more by money than genuine interest.

2. Macro Influencers

With 100,000 to a million followers, macro influencers have often built a reputation as experts or thought leaders in a particular field, such as travel, fitness, fashion, or tech. While they may lack the celebrity appeal of mega influencers, they can offer more targeted engagement. Macro influencers are appealing to brands because they balance reach with niche expertise, creating a stronger connection with their audience.

For instance, a tech brand launching a new smartwatch might partner with a tech-focused macro influencer. This partnership ensures the product reaches a relevant audience interested in tech innovations while maintaining a sense of authenticity, as the influencer is seen as knowledgeable in that field.

3. Micro Influencers

Micro influencers typically have between 10,000 and 100,000 followers and are often regarded as highly relatable figures. They cultivate a dedicated, engaged audience by sharing relatable experiences, advice, and opinions within a specific niche. Micro influencers are particularly valuable to brands because of their ability to foster a sense of community and trust with their followers.

Micro influencers usually engage in more personal interactions with their followers, which increases their credibility. A fitness-focused micro influencer, for example, who consistently posts workout routines and shares her fitness journey, may create a stronger connection with her followers than a celebrity would. Her followers are more likely to trust her product recommendations because they see her as a "friend" or peer, not just a public figure.

4. Nano Influencers

Nano influencers have fewer than 10,000 followers and often engage with a small but highly loyal community. Though they lack reach, they make up for it with a personal touch. Nano influencers have close-knit relationships with their followers, often responding to every comment and message, and creating content that feels genuine and unfiltered.

For brands targeting specific local or niche markets, nano influencers can be incredibly effective. For instance, a local coffee shop may work with a nano influencer who shares her morning coffee routines, reaching an audience in that exact geographic area with a relatable, trusted recommendation.

5. Niche Influencers

Niche influencers may fall into any of the above categories but are distinguished by their focus on highly specific topics. They might center their content around eco-friendly living, plant-based diets, digital art, or DIY home improvement. Brands within these specific spaces can benefit greatly from niche influencers, as their audience is already aligned with the brand's values and products.

Each influencer type has its unique strengths and limitations, and choosing the right type depends on a brand's goals, target audience, and values. For example, a luxury fashion brand launching a new product line may prioritize reach and work with a mega influencer, while a small organic skincare brand might find greater success with micro or nano influencers who share their eco-conscious values.

Section 2: The Evolution of Influencer Marketing

Influencer marketing has evolved significantly over the past decade, moving from traditional celebrity endorsements to a new model where everyday individuals can influence their followers' purchasing decisions.

The Role of Social Media Platforms

Social media platforms have been instrumental in reshaping influencer marketing. Each platform offers different opportunities for influencer engagement:

- **Instagram** is ideal for visual storytelling and lifestyle content, making it a popular choice for influencers in fashion, travel, and food.
- **YouTube** enables long-form content, perfect for tutorials, vlogs, and reviews. YouTube's format allows influencers to create in-depth, educational content that builds trust.
- **TikTok** has introduced a new kind of viral, short-form content. The platform's algorithm often favors authenticity over production quality, allowing influencers to reach large audiences with spontaneous, relatable content.

Each platform has helped shift the focus from traditional celebrities to influencers who are experts or enthusiasts in specific fields. As audiences have moved to social media for product recommendations and lifestyle inspiration, brands have followed suit, leveraging these platforms to connect with consumers in more meaningful ways.

The Rise of the "Everyday" Influencer

With the shift to social media came the rise of the "everyday" influencer—ordinary individuals who, through consistency, engagement, and passion, amassed followings based on their personalities, expertise, and shared experiences. These influencers reflect their audience's lives and aspirations, making their recommendations feel genuine and trustworthy.

The "everyday" influencer phenomenon has given rise to micro and nano influencers who don't have celebrity status but can still drive engagement and impact purchasing decisions. For example, a working mom sharing parenting tips on Instagram might partner with a baby product brand. Her followers, who may share similar lifestyles, will likely trust her recommendation over that of a well-known celebrity.

Impact on Consumer Behavior

Influencer marketing has also transformed consumer behavior. Studies show that a significant number of social media users have made purchases based on influencer recommendations. This influence extends beyond products; influencers often inspire followers to adopt new lifestyles, from fitness routines and dietary changes to travel destinations and sustainability practices. Brands that understand and respect this influence can create campaigns that resonate more deeply with their audiences.

Section 3: Influencer-Consumer Trust

Building Trust in an Era of Skepticism

Trust is the cornerstone of influencer marketing, but with the rise of paid partnerships, audiences have become increasingly skeptical. Today's consumers are media-savvy and can spot insincere endorsements. For brands and influencers to succeed, transparency and authenticity must be at the forefront.

How Influencers Build Credibility

An influencer's credibility is often rooted in several factors:

1. **Consistency**: Influencers who stick to specific content themes build trust by maintaining a clear identity. An influencer dedicated to sustainable living, for instance, will have more credibility promoting eco-friendly products than one who occasionally dabbles in green topics.
2. **Relatability**: Followers connect with influencers who share similar challenges and interests. An influencer who openly shares her fitness journey, struggles, and progress resonates more with followers than a polished celebrity endorsement.
3. **Engagement**: Influencers who respond to comments, interact with followers, and share personal stories build stronger relationships. Followers feel acknowledged and connected, which translates into greater trust.

The Power of Authentic Recommendations

An authentic recommendation is one that feels natural and aligns with the influencer's identity. Audiences are quick to spot inauthenticity and will question endorsements that seem disconnected from the influencer's usual values. Influencers who are selective about brand partnerships tend to maintain their audience's trust by only endorsing products they genuinely believe in.

For example, an influencer focused on health and wellness who promotes a fast-food chain may damage her credibility, as it conflicts with her usual content. In contrast, her endorsement of a natural supplements brand would align better with her personal brand, leading to greater engagement and impact.

Section 4: Why Brands Should Focus on Authentic Partnerships

Influencer marketing can be highly effective, but only when approached thoughtfully. Short-term, transactional partnerships often yield limited results. Brands that focus on authenticity, however, can create impactful, long-term relationships.

Case Studies of Authentic Partnerships

Consider a skincare brand collaborating with a dermatologist influencer who provides honest, science-backed reviews. This partnership not only brings credibility to the brand but also creates genuine value for the audience, as they're receiving expert advice. Another example is a fitness brand partnering with an influencer who shares personal fitness journeys, building an organic connection with her audience.

Benefits of Long-Term Influencer Relationships

Long-term partnerships allow influencers to fully integrate a brand into their content, creating more authentic messaging. They also foster loyalty and trust, making audiences more receptive to the brand over time. When brands invest in these relationships, they not only gain visibility but also build a stronger reputation and brand affinity among the influencer's followers.

Conclusion: Setting the Stage for Success

The modern influencer landscape is diverse, and understanding its complexities is essential for brands seeking meaningful, lasting impact. By choosing the right influencers, respecting the importance of authenticity, and focusing on long-term relationships, brands can move beyond superficial partnerships. These strategies will help brands connect with audiences on a deeper level, building trust, engagement, and loyalty in the process.

Chapter 2: Defining Authenticity in Partnerships

Introduction

Authenticity is one of the most vital elements in today's influencer marketing landscape. With the proliferation of sponsored posts and paid partnerships, consumers are increasingly able to distinguish genuine endorsements from those that feel forced or insincere. In an age where audiences are more skeptical than ever, authenticity isn't just a buzzword—it's a business imperative. This chapter examines what it means to create authentic partnerships, the characteristics of genuine influencer collaborations, and how brands can avoid the pitfalls of superficial alliances.

By understanding and embracing authenticity, brands can build lasting, impactful relationships with influencers that resonate with their audiences. This chapter will also explore red flags to avoid and illustrate how authenticity directly impacts engagement, trust, and loyalty.

Section 1: Beyond Numbers—What Authenticity Really Means

Authenticity in influencer marketing is about more than simply achieving high engagement rates or boosting visibility. While metrics are essential, focusing solely on quantitative data can lead brands to overlook the qualitative elements that build lasting trust. Authentic partnerships are those that align with the values, lifestyle, and persona of the influencer and, by extension, resonate with their audience on a deeper level.

What Authenticity Looks Like in Influencer Marketing

1. **Genuine Brand-Influencer Alignment**: Authenticity starts with alignment. When a brand's mission and values mirror those of the influencer, the partnership naturally feels genuine. Followers notice when influencers endorse brands that genuinely fit into their lives versus brands that don't.
2. **Transparent Sponsorships**: Transparency is central to authenticity. Audiences are more likely to trust influencers who disclose sponsored content openly. When influencers are upfront about their partnerships, they respect their audience's intelligence and build trust over time.
3. **Consistent Message and Brand Fit**: Authenticity thrives on consistency. A beauty influencer who consistently talks about natural and organic products, for example, maintains her credibility when she endorses a cruelty-free skincare brand. Her audience

understands that she's staying true to her values, and the endorsement doesn't feel like a departure from her usual content.

4. **Influencer Control and Creative Freedom**: When influencers have creative freedom, they're able to produce content that feels natural to their style. Authentic partnerships allow influencers to communicate in their unique voices rather than following a strict script. When influencers are encouraged to craft their own stories around a brand, the result is a campaign that feels honest, relatable, and credible.

5. **Long-Term Relationships Over One-Off Campaigns**: Authentic partnerships are rarely built through one-off collaborations. Long-term relationships allow influencers to integrate a brand into their lives, creating a natural and sustained endorsement that feels more genuine to audiences. When an influencer repeatedly endorses a brand over time, it signals genuine enthusiasm, strengthening audience trust.

Examples of Authentic Partnerships

Take, for example, a food influencer with a focus on sustainable eating who partners with an eco-friendly grocery delivery service. This partnership is a natural extension of the influencer's established identity, values, and content. The audience perceives it as a seamless collaboration, as the brand aligns with what the influencer already advocates.

Another example might be a travel blogger known for sharing budget-friendly travel tips partnering with an affordable airline or hotel chain. Followers likely see the partnership as a reflection of the influencer's commitment to accessible travel, reinforcing the influencer's authenticity.

Section 2: Red Flags in Influencer Partnerships

In influencer marketing, there are several signs that can indicate an inauthentic partnership, and recognizing these red flags can help brands avoid superficial collaborations that could damage their credibility and reputation.

1. Brand Mismatches

One of the most noticeable red flags is a brand mismatch. When an influencer's partnership with a brand feels out of character, audiences can quickly pick up on the disconnect. For instance, if a wellness influencer who consistently advocates for a vegan lifestyle suddenly promotes a fast-food chain known for its meat products, followers may question her motives, and the endorsement could backfire.

2. Forced or Scripted Content

Forced or overly scripted content is another red flag. Audiences are generally receptive to authentic, natural language, and when influencers are restricted by rigid scripts, the content may feel contrived. Followers tend to be highly attuned to an influencer's typical tone, and a sudden shift to promotional language can reduce credibility.

3. High Frequency of Sponsored Content

While paid partnerships are common, an excessive amount of sponsored content can erode an influencer's credibility. When every post seems to be an endorsement, followers may question the influencer's authenticity and wonder if they're prioritizing financial gain over genuine recommendations. Brands should look for influencers who balance sponsored content with organic posts to maintain a sense of authenticity.

4. Lack of Engagement

An influencer's engagement with followers is often a key indicator of authenticity. If an influencer rarely interacts with comments or doesn't seem invested in their audience's questions or concerns, it can signal a lack of genuine connection. Authentic influencers usually take time to answer questions, respond to comments, and engage in conversations with their followers, demonstrating that they genuinely value their audience.

5. Rapid Changes in Brand Partnerships

Frequent changes in brand partnerships, especially within the same product category, can create doubts about an influencer's authenticity. If a beauty influencer endorses one skincare brand in January and switches to a competitor in February, it sends mixed signals to followers. Rapid shifts between competing brands can give the impression that endorsements are driven by financial motives rather than personal belief in the products.

Case Study: The Consequences of Inauthentic Partnerships

Consider a high-profile case involving an influencer who faced backlash after promoting a diet product that contradicted her usual body-positive messaging. Her followers criticized the partnership, pointing out that it conflicted with the values she typically represented. The backlash was significant, leading to a loss of followers and damage to her credibility. This case serves as a cautionary example, highlighting how inauthentic partnerships can have long-lasting negative consequences.

Section 3: How to Spot and Build Authenticity in Influencer Partnerships

Brands seeking authentic partnerships need to establish a set of criteria for identifying influencers who align with their values and mission. This process involves careful selection, open communication, and a commitment to authenticity on both sides.

1. Research and Selection

Choosing the right influencer is more complex than reviewing follower counts and engagement rates. Brands should conduct thorough research into an influencer's content, tone, and values. Understanding an influencer's background, interests, and audience demographics can reveal whether they're a good fit for the brand.

Tools like audience analysis software can help brands assess an influencer's follower demographics, engagement quality, and authenticity metrics. By studying an influencer's historical content, brands can gain insights into how well they align with the brand's identity.

2. Open Communication and Expectation Setting

Transparency and communication are essential to building authentic partnerships. Brands should set clear expectations from the start, but they should also invite influencers to share their input on how they can best represent the brand in a way that feels natural. Open dialogue can lead to creative, authentic content ideas that align with the influencer's style and the brand's goals.

3. Embracing Influencer Feedback

Authentic partnerships work best when influencers feel empowered to provide feedback on the brand and products. Brands that are open to feedback can benefit from the influencer's unique insights into their audience, creating a campaign that is both engaging and effective. When influencers genuinely believe in the products they endorse, their enthusiasm comes through in their content, making the endorsement feel more natural.

4. Focusing on Relationship Building

Instead of one-off partnerships, brands should aim to build long-term relationships with influencers. Long-term relationships allow influencers to integrate the brand into their lives more organically, creating a sustained narrative that followers trust. Repeated endorsements signal to the audience that the influencer truly believes in the brand, which fosters a sense of authenticity and loyalty.

Case Study: Building an Authentic Partnership Over Time

A successful example of long-term brand-influencer partnership is the collaboration between a prominent fitness influencer and an athletic apparel brand. Over several years, the influencer has consistently promoted the brand, sharing personal stories of how the products fit into her fitness journey. Her followers see her as a genuine advocate, and the sustained partnership has led to increased trust and loyalty among her audience.

Section 4: The Long-Term Impact of Authenticity

When brands and influencers embrace authenticity, the rewards extend beyond short-term gains. Authentic partnerships help brands foster trust, build brand loyalty, and create meaningful connections with consumers that lead to sustained growth. Influencers who genuinely align with a brand's values act as true advocates, and their passion resonates with followers on a deeper level.

Brand Loyalty and Consumer Trust

Authentic partnerships can lead to higher levels of brand loyalty and trust. When followers believe in the sincerity of an influencer's endorsement, they're more likely to develop a connection with the brand itself. This connection can foster long-term loyalty, as followers feel a sense of trust and familiarity with the brand.

Positive Brand Perception

When brands prioritize authenticity, they also benefit from positive public perception. Consumers are more likely to view brands that embrace authenticity as transparent and trustworthy, which strengthens the brand's reputation in the market.

Competitive Advantage

Brands that build authentic influencer partnerships often stand out from competitors. As consumers increasingly seek authenticity, brands that prioritize genuine partnerships are better positioned to attract loyal customers who appreciate transparent and honest marketing.

Conclusion: The Value of Authenticity

Defining and embracing authenticity is essential in today's influencer marketing landscape. By focusing on genuine partnerships that align with the influencer's identity, values, and audience, brands can create more meaningful connections with consumers. Authentic partnerships build trust, foster loyalty, and create a lasting impact that goes beyond immediate metrics. When brands commit to authenticity, they set the foundation for influencer relationships that are both powerful and enduring.

With a clear understanding of what authenticity entails and how to foster it in partnerships, brands are better equipped to navigate the influencer landscape with integrity and success.

Chapter 3: Aligning Brand Values and Influencer Persona

Introduction

The key to a successful influencer marketing campaign lies in alignment—specifically, aligning the values and persona of the influencer with the core identity of the brand. In a landscape where consumers are more discerning than ever, superficial partnerships often fail to resonate, while thoughtful collaborations can create meaningful connections that drive long-term loyalty. In this chapter, we'll explore how brands can identify influencers who genuinely align with their values, why this alignment matters, and the ways in which brands can create partnerships that feel natural, credible, and powerful.

By choosing influencers whose values reflect their own, brands build relationships that feel authentic to audiences, fostering trust and deepening engagement. This chapter will discuss the steps brands should take to achieve this alignment and offer real-world examples of how value-driven partnerships can drive sustained success.

Section 1: Understanding Brand Values

Before brands can seek alignment with influencers, they need to define their own core values and identity. Brand values go beyond a company's product offerings; they encompass the beliefs, principles, and vision that shape how a brand interacts with the world.

Defining Core Brand Values

Core brand values are the principles that guide a company's operations, messaging, and purpose. They answer questions like, *What does this brand stand for? What does it aspire to achieve beyond profitability?* For instance, a sustainable fashion brand might prioritize environmental stewardship, fair labor practices, and transparency. These values inform everything from material sourcing to brand messaging, and they set the foundation for authentic influencer partnerships.

For brands that have yet to clearly define these values, starting with a mission statement and vision can be helpful. A mission statement answers the question *Why do we exist?* and a vision addresses *What do we want to achieve in the future?* Together, these guiding principles form the backbone of the brand, serving as a benchmark against which potential influencer partners can be evaluated.

How Brand Values Impact Consumer Perception

Today's consumers are often more inclined to purchase from brands that align with their personal values. A survey by Accenture found that over 60% of consumers want brands to take a stand on social, cultural, environmental, and political issues. Brand values not only shape consumer perception but also attract like-minded influencers who can authentically represent the brand's vision and mission. When consumers see an influencer who shares similar values endorsing a brand, the partnership feels more credible, increasing the likelihood of a positive response.

Section 2: Defining Influencer Persona and Values

An influencer's persona goes beyond their content style; it reflects their character, interests, lifestyle, and values. To find an influencer who aligns with brand values, it's essential to analyze both their persona and their core beliefs. Followers gravitate toward influencers they trust and respect, and when an influencer authentically represents a brand, that trust extends to the brand as well.

Understanding Influencer Persona

An influencer's persona is their public-facing identity on social media. It's shaped by their tone, style, interests, and the topics they discuss. Influencers often create content around specific themes, such as fitness, travel, fashion, wellness, or personal development. Their persona also includes how they interact with their audience, handle partnerships, and share personal stories.

A fitness influencer, for example, may have a persona centered on empowerment, discipline, and wellness. They might share workout routines, nutritional advice, and personal insights on mental health. Their followers likely view them as a trusted source for health-related information, and they expect their endorsements to align with these values.

Identifying Influencer Values

An influencer's values may not always be explicit, but they can often be discerned by analyzing their content, past partnerships, and the causes they support. For instance, an influencer who frequently discusses climate change, uses eco-friendly products, and promotes sustainable practices likely values environmental responsibility. Brands should examine an influencer's historical content and past endorsements to understand their values better. Influencers with a track record of supporting causes or brands that align with the brand's core values are more likely to represent the brand authentically.

Red Flags: When Values Don't Align

Brands should be cautious of influencers whose values seem to clash with the brand's. For instance, if a luxury brand that emphasizes exclusivity and craftsmanship partners with an influencer known for promoting fast fashion, the partnership may feel dissonant to both parties' audiences. A mismatch can damage the credibility of both the influencer and the brand, leading to negative feedback from consumers who expect consistency in both brands' messaging.

Section 3: Steps to Achieve Brand-Influencer Alignment

Achieving true alignment between brand values and influencer persona requires a strategic, thoughtful approach. Here's a step-by-step process brands can follow to ensure they're creating authentic, value-driven partnerships:

1. Define and Clarify Brand Objectives

Before beginning the search for an influencer, brands need to clarify their objectives for the partnership. What do they hope to achieve? Whether it's brand awareness, increased sales, or audience engagement, having clear objectives will help guide the type of influencer best suited to represent the brand. The goals will also shape the selection criteria, as different objectives may call for different types of influencers. For instance, a brand launching an eco-friendly product line might seek an influencer who advocates for sustainability to reinforce their message.

2. Conduct In-Depth Research on Potential Influencers

Once objectives are established, the next step is thorough research. Brands should look for influencers whose content, tone, and audience align with their values. This process involves more than reviewing follower counts and engagement rates; brands should examine the influencer's content history, tone, past partnerships, and overall reputation.

Tools like social listening platforms and influencer databases can provide valuable insights into an influencer's audience demographics, engagement patterns, and past brand collaborations. Brands can also analyze comments, reviews, and testimonials to understand how the influencer's audience perceives them and gauge how well they might resonate with the brand's target audience.

3. Analyze Engagement Quality

The quality of an influencer's engagement is often a better indicator of alignment than their follower count. Influencers who regularly interact with their followers, respond to comments, and engage in discussions tend to have higher credibility and trustworthiness. High-quality engagement indicates that the influencer has a strong relationship with their audience, which is essential for delivering a brand message that feels authentic.

4. Open a Dialogue About Values and Expectations

Once a potential influencer partner has been identified, brands should initiate a conversation about values, expectations, and creative freedom. By discussing values openly, both parties can assess whether they're genuinely aligned. This dialogue also provides an opportunity for influencers to share how they envision integrating the brand into their content, ensuring the partnership feels authentic and seamless.

Brands should be transparent about their expectations, but they should also respect the influencer's creative voice. Authenticity thrives when influencers have creative freedom to present the brand in a way that feels natural to them.

5. Start with a Trial Collaboration

A trial collaboration can be a great way to test alignment without committing to a long-term partnership immediately. By starting with a one-off campaign or product placement, brands can assess how well the influencer represents their values and gauge audience reaction. If the trial partnership is successful, brands can then consider building a long-term relationship with the influencer.

Case Study: Aligning Brand Values in Practice

One well-known example of a successful value-aligned partnership is the collaboration between the sustainable footwear brand Allbirds and environmental advocates. Allbirds' mission is rooted in sustainability, and they've partnered with influencers who share a passion for environmental responsibility. These influencers don't just promote the products; they also educate their followers about Allbirds' eco-friendly materials and ethical practices. The partnership feels genuine, as it aligns with both the brand's and influencers' commitment to sustainability.

Section 4: Benefits of Strong Brand-Influencer Alignment

When brands and influencers share aligned values, the benefits go beyond short-term engagement. Authentic alignment fosters trust, deepens brand loyalty, and drives long-term impact.

1. Enhanced Credibility and Trust

An influencer who genuinely believes in a brand's mission communicates that belief to their followers, creating a sense of trust. This authenticity boosts the brand's credibility, as followers see the endorsement as more than just a transaction. For example, when a wellness influencer advocates for a natural skincare brand that aligns with her values of self-care and natural living, her followers are more likely to trust the recommendation.

2. Stronger Audience Engagement

Aligned partnerships often lead to higher engagement rates. Followers are more receptive to content that feels organic and relevant, and when they see an influencer genuinely integrating a brand into their life, they're more likely to engage with the content. A fashion influencer who believes in sustainable fashion and collaborates with a slow-fashion brand can create engaging content that resonates deeply with followers who share similar values.

3. Increased Brand Loyalty

When consumers feel that a brand shares their values, they're more likely to become loyal customers. Aligned influencer partnerships reinforce this sense of shared purpose, creating long-lasting relationships between the brand and its audience. Over time, these partnerships build a loyal customer base that associates the brand with authenticity, integrity, and trustworthiness.

4. Positive Brand Perception and Reputation

When brands prioritize value alignment, they benefit from positive public perception. Consumers view brands that emphasize authenticity as transparent and socially responsible, strengthening the brand's reputation. Aligned partnerships with trusted influencers contribute to a brand image that consumers admire, fostering goodwill and positive word-of-mouth.

Conclusion: Creating Partnerships with Purpose

Aligning brand values and influencer persona is essential for building partnerships that feel natural, credible, and impactful. When brands invest in understanding both their own values and those of potential influencer partners, they can create campaigns that go beyond surface-level metrics to build real connections. Value-driven partnerships not only enhance credibility but also drive meaningful engagement, trust, and loyalty.

In an influencer marketing landscape that prioritizes quick wins, brands that focus on long-term, value-aligned relationships stand to gain a significant competitive advantage. Authenticity and alignment are the cornerstones of sustainable success, and by creating partnerships with purpose, brands can foster connections that leave a lasting impact on audiences.

Chapter 4: Identifying the Right Influencers

Introduction

Choosing the right influencer is one of the most critical steps in executing a successful influencer marketing campaign. With countless influencers across various platforms, brands need a strategic approach to identify the individuals who can effectively represent their brand's values, reach the target audience, and build authentic connections. In this chapter, we'll discuss the steps to identifying the right influencers, from understanding audience demographics to evaluating engagement quality, and we'll introduce tools and techniques to streamline the search process.

Selecting the right influencers is about more than looking at follower counts or engagement rates. Brands need to consider alignment, audience fit, and potential impact, ensuring that the influencer partnership will yield meaningful results. This chapter will guide brands through a thorough selection process, helping them build a foundation for impactful partnerships.

Section 1: Determining the Right Type of Influencer for Your Brand

Before diving into the search, brands should determine the type of influencer who best suits their goals. Each influencer category—mega, macro, micro, and nano—has unique advantages and limitations. By understanding these distinctions, brands can narrow their search to find influencers who align with their objectives.

1. Mega Influencers for Mass Visibility

Mega influencers, often with over a million followers, are best suited for brands seeking broad visibility. These influencers include celebrities and public figures whose reach spans diverse demographics, making them ideal for large-scale awareness campaigns. However, because of their vast reach, their engagement may be lower than influencers with smaller, more niche audiences. Brands with extensive budgets and mainstream appeal often benefit from working with mega influencers to build widespread brand recognition.

2. Macro Influencers for Targeted Reach and Influence

Macro influencers, with follower counts typically between 100,000 and a million, offer a balance of reach and niche influence. They're often experts or thought leaders in specific areas like fitness, fashion, travel, or technology. Brands that want to reach a broad audience within a particular interest group can benefit from partnering with macro influencers, as they provide both reach and relevance.

3. Micro Influencers for Higher Engagement and Community Building (continued)

Micro influencers are highly effective for brands aiming to build strong relationships with their audience. Due to their smaller following, they tend to engage more personally with their followers, creating a sense of community. This category is particularly beneficial for brands with niche products or services, as micro influencers can deliver more intimate and genuine endorsements that resonate deeply with their followers. These partnerships are typically more budget-friendly than those with macro or mega influencers, making them accessible for small to medium-sized businesses.

4. Nano Influencers for Hyper-Targeted and Local Campaigns

Nano influencers, those with fewer than 10,000 followers, engage with small, close-knit communities. While they may lack the reach of other categories, nano influencers often have the most personal relationships with their audience, resulting in high levels of trust. Brands looking to target specific local markets, test new products, or reach niche audiences benefit from nano influencers' unique ability to communicate authentically with their followers. Nano influencers are also a cost-effective option, making them ideal for grassroots campaigns that require a high level of authenticity and community engagement.

Selecting the Right Influencer Category for Your Goals

By defining campaign objectives—whether for mass visibility, niche influence, community engagement, or hyper-local targeting—brands can better understand which influencer type is best suited to their needs. Clarifying these goals early in the campaign planning process ensures that the influencer selection process aligns with the brand's overarching strategy.

Section 2: Understanding Your Target Audience

Once the appropriate influencer category is determined, the next step is understanding the brand's target audience. A deep understanding of audience demographics and interests is essential to ensure influencer alignment and campaign success.

1. Audience Demographics

Demographic factors like age, gender, location, income level, and lifestyle play a significant role in influencer selection. For example, a skincare brand targeting young, eco-conscious women would benefit from partnering with a beauty influencer whose audience aligns with these demographics. Using tools like Google Analytics, social media insights, and third-party audience analysis tools, brands can identify their target demographics and use this data to guide the influencer selection process.

2. Audience Interests and Values

Demographics alone aren't enough—brands need to understand the interests, behaviors, and values of their audience. What matters most to your audience? Are they interested in sustainable products, wellness, technology, or fashion? Do they prioritize ethical sourcing, or are they driven more by cost-effectiveness? Analyzing audience interests helps brands connect with influencers whose followers share similar values, increasing the likelihood of authentic engagement and positive brand perception.

3. Platform-Specific Preferences

Understanding where the target audience spends their time is crucial. Each social media platform attracts different demographics and usage behaviors. For instance:

- **Instagram** is popular among younger audiences and is known for its visual content, making it ideal for beauty, fashion, and lifestyle brands.

- **YouTube** attracts audiences interested in long-form content and tutorials, suitable for brands that benefit from detailed product explanations, such as technology or skincare.
- **TikTok** appeals to Gen Z with short, entertaining content, perfect for brands targeting a younger, trend-driven audience.

By identifying which platforms the target audience frequents, brands can focus their influencer search on individuals who are most active and influential on those channels.

Section 3: Evaluating Influencer Metrics Beyond Follower Count

Once potential influencers have been identified, it's essential to evaluate them based on metrics beyond just follower count. While a high follower count can indicate reach, it doesn't guarantee engagement or alignment. Here are some critical metrics to consider:

1. Engagement Rate

Engagement rate is often a more valuable metric than follower count, as it reflects the influencer's ability to connect with their audience. A high engagement rate indicates that followers are actively interacting with the content, showing interest and trust. Engagement can be measured by the ratio of likes, comments, and shares to the number of followers. For example, an influencer with 50,000 followers and a 5% engagement rate might drive more impact than an influencer with 200,000 followers and a 1% engagement rate.

2. Quality of Engagement

Engagement quality goes beyond numbers and involves analyzing the nature of interactions. Genuine comments and questions from followers show a higher level of trust and interest than simple emoji reactions or generic comments. When evaluating influencers, brands should look at the tone and content of follower interactions. Are followers asking for product recommendations, sharing personal experiences, or providing feedback? These types of interactions suggest a highly engaged audience that's more likely to trust the influencer's endorsements.

3. Authenticity and Consistency

Consistency in posting frequency and brand alignment also play a critical role in influencer selection. Influencers who regularly post high-quality content and maintain a consistent theme are more likely to represent brands effectively. Brands should review an influencer's historical posts to ensure their content, values, and tone align with the brand's image. Consistent influencers who have built their audience over time tend to have more loyal followers and are perceived as more authentic.

4. Audience Sentiment

Audience sentiment analysis involves evaluating the tone and mood of followers' responses to the influencer's posts. Positive sentiment suggests that followers view the influencer favorably, making them more receptive to their recommendations. Conversely, negative sentiment may indicate a lack of trust or dissatisfaction, which could affect the success of the partnership. Social listening tools can help brands assess sentiment trends and ensure they're partnering with influencers who resonate well with their audience.

5. Past Brand Partnerships and Endorsements

An influencer's history with past brand partnerships can provide insight into how they handle collaborations and endorsements. Reviewing an influencer's previous campaigns helps brands understand their approach to sponsored content, creative flexibility, and alignment with similar brands. If an influencer has worked with brands with values that align with your own, it may suggest they'd be a good fit for your campaign. However, if they've promoted competing brands within a short period, it might indicate a less genuine approach to endorsements.

Section 4: Tools and Techniques for Influencer Discovery

Identifying the right influencer can be a complex task, but a range of tools and techniques can help brands streamline the process and make data-driven decisions. Here are some of the top tools and methods for influencer discovery:

1. Social Listening Tools

Social listening tools like Sprout Social, Brandwatch, and Hootsuite Insights enable brands to track keywords, hashtags, and conversations relevant to their industry. By monitoring trends and discussions, brands can identify influential voices who naturally engage with their target topics and audiences. Social listening can also reveal micro and nano influencers who are active in niche areas, providing opportunities for hyper-targeted partnerships.

2. Influencer Databases

Influencer databases, such as Upfluence, AspireIQ, and Traackr, offer searchable directories of influencers with filters based on follower count, engagement rate, audience demographics, and more. These tools allow brands to narrow down their search and identify influencers who meet specific criteria, such as location, niche, and engagement quality. Many influencer databases also provide insights into audience demographics, helping brands ensure alignment with their target audience.

3. Platform-Specific Insights

Each social media platform provides built-in analytics that can be useful for influencer discovery. Instagram, for example, offers insights into engagement metrics, audience demographics, and follower growth. YouTube provides data on video views, audience retention, and top traffic sources. Brands can use these platform insights to assess influencer performance and audience alignment on specific channels.

4. Hashtag and Keyword Research

Hashtag and keyword research is a valuable technique for discovering influencers who are already engaging with relevant topics. By tracking industry-specific hashtags and keywords, brands can identify influencers who are actively contributing to conversations related to their niche. For example, a fitness brand might search for hashtags like #FitnessMotivation or #WellnessTips to find influencers in the health and wellness space.

5. Competitor Analysis

Analyzing competitors' influencer partnerships can offer insights into potential collaborators within the industry. By studying the influencers that competitors work with, brands can identify individuals who resonate well with similar audiences. Competitor analysis can also highlight gaps in the market where brands can differentiate themselves by working with influencers in unexplored niches.

Section 5: Building an Influencer Shortlist and Making the Final Selection

After conducting initial research and analysis, brands should create a shortlist of influencers who meet their criteria. This shortlist serves as a foundation for further evaluation and enables brands to make the final selection with confidence.

1. Final Evaluation Criteria

Once a shortlist is created, brands should re-evaluate each influencer against specific criteria, such as audience alignment, engagement quality, and brand fit. Brands can also conduct test collaborations with shortlisted influencers, such as small product placements or one-off campaigns, to gauge audience response and effectiveness before committing to a long-term partnership.

2. Communication and Collaboration

Reaching out to shortlisted influencers with clear expectations and open communication is essential for setting the stage for a successful partnership. By discussing objectives, creative freedom, and brand values upfront, brands and influencers can establish a shared vision for the campaign. This initial dialogue also helps both parties gauge compatibility and ensure the partnership feels mutually beneficial and authentic.

3. Legal and Contractual Considerations

Before finalizing an influencer partnership, brands should address legal and contractual elements, such as content ownership, exclusivity, and disclosure requirements. Ensuring that both parties understand and agree on these terms is essential to avoid misunderstandings and maintain transparency throughout the campaign.

Conclusion: Setting the Stage for Effective Partnerships

Identifying the right influencers is a nuanced process that requires careful consideration of various factors, from audience demographics to engagement quality and value alignment. By following a structured approach and leveraging tools for influencer discovery, brands can find influencers who authentically represent their mission and connect meaningfully with their target audience.

With the right influencers in place, brands lay a solid foundation for impactful, lasting partnerships that go beyond surface-level engagement to build trust, foster loyalty, and drive sustained success. This thorough selection process sets the stage for future chapters, where we'll explore strategies for building and maintaining effective partnerships that yield long-term results.

Chapter 5: Building Relationships with Influencers

Introduction

In influencer marketing, success often hinges on the strength of the relationship between the brand and the influencer. While one-off campaigns can create a short-lived impact, cultivating a long-term, collaborative relationship with influencers fosters loyalty, authenticity, and deeper connections with their audience. By viewing influencers as strategic partners rather than mere content creators, brands can unlock the full potential of these collaborations, ensuring both the brand and influencer grow together in mutually beneficial ways.

This chapter delves into strategies for building and nurturing strong relationships with influencers, focusing on the importance of trust, effective communication, and providing influencers with the creative freedom they need to authentically represent the brand. From understanding influencers' needs and motivations to developing long-term partnerships, this chapter provides actionable steps for establishing productive, lasting influencer relationships.

Section 1: Laying the Foundation for Successful Partnerships

A strong relationship with an influencer begins with a solid foundation based on respect, trust, and alignment. This foundation is built not only on choosing the right influencers, as we discussed in Chapter 4, but also on approaching them with a collaborative mindset that values their unique perspective and contributions.

1. Setting Clear, Aligned Objectives

The first step to any successful influencer partnership is to establish clear, aligned objectives. Both the brand and the influencer should be on the same page regarding the purpose of the partnership, whether it's to drive brand awareness, increase engagement, generate sales, or educate an audience on a specific issue.

Collaborating on goal-setting encourages mutual investment and helps both parties stay committed to the partnership's success. Brands should consider asking influencers about their personal goals and aspirations to ensure that the campaign's objectives align with their vision. For example, if an influencer is passionate about sustainability, aligning the partnership around eco-friendly initiatives can foster a deeper commitment to the brand and a more genuine endorsement.

2. Providing Fair Compensation

Compensation is a fundamental aspect of establishing a respectful, long-term relationship.

Influencers put significant effort, time, and resources into creating content that resonates with their audience, and they should be compensated fairly for their work. While rates vary depending on an influencer's reach, engagement, and niche, compensation should reflect the value the influencer brings to the partnership.

Transparent and fair compensation discussions also reinforce trust, showing influencers that the brand values their contributions. Brands can offer a range of compensation options, from upfront payments and performance-based incentives to affiliate commissions and product collaborations. Offering creative compensation models can be especially appealing to influencers, giving them a sense of ownership in the partnership's success.

3. Recognizing Influencers as Creative Partners

To build a strong foundation, brands should recognize influencers as creative partners who bring unique insights, skills, and perspectives. This approach requires viewing influencers as more than just promoters; they're valuable storytellers with in-depth knowledge of what resonates with their audience. Brands should trust influencers to communicate the brand message in their own voice, style, and tone.

By giving influencers creative freedom, brands allow them to craft content that feels organic and genuine, fostering authenticity. For instance, rather than dictating specific language or visuals, a beauty brand might outline key product benefits but let the influencer design the content around their unique routine or personal story.

Section 2: Building Trust and Loyalty in Influencer Relationships

Trust is the cornerstone of any successful influencer-brand relationship. Without trust, influencers may feel restricted, leading to content that feels forced or inauthentic. Building trust requires transparency, consistent communication, and respect for the influencer's autonomy.

1. Transparency and Open Communication

Transparency is critical for establishing trust. Brands should be open about their expectations, campaign goals, and any limitations, while influencers should feel comfortable sharing their creative vision, concerns, and feedback. Clear communication helps prevent misunderstandings, ensuring both parties remain aligned throughout the partnership.

Regular check-ins can strengthen trust, especially during long-term collaborations. Brands might schedule periodic calls or meetings to discuss campaign performance, address any issues, and brainstorm new ideas. Keeping these lines of communication open makes influencers feel valued and empowered, reinforcing their commitment to the brand.

2. Honoring Creative Freedom

Influencers thrive on creative freedom, and respecting their creative process is essential to building loyalty. While brands may want specific messages conveyed, strict control over the influencer's content can stifle authenticity, reducing the effectiveness of the partnership. Giving influencers the flexibility to produce content in their unique style allows them to integrate the brand seamlessly into their personal narrative.

For example, rather than providing a prescriptive list of talking points, a fitness brand might suggest key themes, like the benefits of a new product, and then let the influencer incorporate these into a workout routine. The influencer's audience is more likely to engage with content that feels natural, increasing the overall impact of the campaign.

3. Long-Term Partnerships vs. One-Off Collaborations

While short-term partnerships can yield quick results, long-term relationships offer a greater return on investment by building trust and credibility over time. Audiences are more receptive to repeated endorsements, as they signal the influencer's genuine affinity for the brand. Long-term partnerships also allow brands and influencers to build a deeper connection, resulting in more meaningful, authentic content.

For example, a skincare brand working with an influencer over several months can showcase the influencer's real journey with the product, sharing progress and updates that add credibility. This approach builds trust, as the influencer's audience sees consistent, honest testimonials rather than fleeting endorsements.

4. Celebrating Milestones Together

Acknowledging and celebrating partnership milestones can strengthen the bond between brands and influencers. Recognizing achievements, such as reaching a sales goal or launching a new product, creates a sense of shared success and motivates influencers to continue investing in the partnership.

Brands might consider sending thank-you notes, gifts, or even hosting events to celebrate these milestones. Personalized gestures show influencers that the brand values their contributions and sees them as integral members of the team. These celebrations help nurture loyalty, making influencers feel appreciated and more inclined to prioritize the brand.

Section 3: Empowering Influencers with Resources and Support

Empowering influencers with the resources they need to succeed can significantly enhance the quality of content they produce, while also demonstrating the brand's commitment to the partnership.

1. Providing Access to Product Knowledge

A key factor in empowering influencers is ensuring they have comprehensive product knowledge. When influencers understand a product's features, benefits, and unique selling points, they can create more informative and persuasive content. Brands can offer influencers product demos, detailed fact sheets, and access to product specialists to ensure they're equipped to answer audience questions and highlight key features.

For example, a technology brand working with a tech influencer might provide a dedicated product expert to explain how a new gadget works. This expertise enables the influencer to offer in-depth reviews, making their endorsements more credible and valuable to their audience.

2. Offering Creative Assets and Guidelines

While creative freedom is essential, providing influencers with helpful assets—such as brand logos, image templates, or suggested hashtags—can enhance the quality of their content while maintaining brand consistency. Clear guidelines help influencers stay aligned with the brand's messaging without compromising their creativity. However, these guidelines should be flexible, allowing influencers to adapt them to their unique style.

For instance, a fashion brand could provide seasonal lookbooks or behind-the-scenes footage from a new collection launch. This material gives influencers additional content to share, enriching their posts and strengthening the partnership's visual identity.

3. Providing Performance Feedback

Offering feedback on performance metrics can be highly beneficial for influencers, helping them understand what resonates with the brand and audience. Metrics such as engagement rates, click-throughs, and conversions provide valuable insights that can inform future content. Constructive feedback not only improves content quality but also shows influencers that the brand values their contributions and is invested in their growth.

Brands should approach feedback with transparency and encouragement, sharing both successes and areas for improvement. A collaborative approach to feedback encourages influencers to refine their strategies, enhancing their impact and effectiveness over time.

Section 4: Creating a Collaborative Environment for Content Creation

Creating a collaborative environment is essential for developing content that feels organic and aligned with both the brand and the influencer's style. Collaboration allows both parties to contribute ideas, brainstorm creative concepts, and experiment with different approaches to maximize impact.

1. Brainstorming Content Ideas Together

Co-creating content ideas helps align the influencer's creative vision with the brand's goals. Brands can hold brainstorming sessions to discuss potential content themes, share campaign ideas, and encourage the influencer's input. By fostering a collaborative approach, brands tap into the influencer's insights and expertise, ensuring the content resonates with their audience.

For example, a travel brand might brainstorm with an influencer on how to showcase a new destination through different types of content—like packing tips, local cuisine highlights, and scenic imagery. This approach generates diverse content, maximizing engagement and impact.

2. Encouraging Influencer-Led Campaigns

Encouraging influencer-led campaigns is another way to foster a sense of ownership in the partnership. When influencers have the freedom to lead and design a campaign, they're more invested in its success. Influencer-led campaigns also showcase the influencer's creativity and personal connection to the brand, resulting in content that feels less scripted and more authentic.

Brands might give influencers control over the campaign's narrative, asking them to integrate a new product or service into a story or experience they share with their audience. For instance, a wellness brand could encourage an influencer to create a "self-care day" featuring their products, with the influencer designing the entire experience around their personal preferences.

3. Allowing Room for Experimentation

Experimentation fosters innovation and allows influencers to discover new ways to engage their audience. By encouraging influencers to experiment with different content formats—such as live streams, short-form videos, or interactive stories—brands allow them to adapt to changing trends and preferences. Room for experimentation keeps content fresh and engaging, helping brands stay relevant in an evolving digital landscape.

For instance, a beauty brand might collaborate with an influencer on a live Q&A session about skincare routines. This format not only allows the influencer to showcase their expertise but also provides an interactive experience for followers, enhancing engagement and interest in the brand.

4. Supporting Influencer Growth and Development

When brands actively support influencers' growth, they create a relationship that feels mutually beneficial. Brands can support influencers by offering training, insights into industry trends, and access to tools that help them improve their content creation skills. Investing in influencers' growth strengthens loyalty and positions the brand as a supportive partner, enhancing the long-term value of the partnership.

For example, a fashion brand might provide influencers with exclusive invitations to industry events or workshops on photography and styling. These opportunities enhance influencers' skills, enabling them to create better content while also reinforcing their connection to the brand.

Section 5: Measuring Success and Celebrating Achievements

Tracking the success of influencer partnerships is essential to understand what works, optimize future campaigns, and celebrate joint achievements. By establishing metrics, analyzing performance, and celebrating successes, brands reinforce the value of the partnership and motivate influencers to continue delivering high-quality content.

1. Establishing Clear KPIs and Performance Metrics

Setting clear key performance indicators (KPIs) at the start of the partnership helps both parties track progress and measure success. KPIs can include metrics such as engagement rates, reach, conversions, or sales generated through the campaign. Establishing these goals upfront allows brands and influencers to focus on what matters most and track impact effectively.

2. Reviewing Campaign Performance Together

Brands should review campaign performance with influencers regularly, discussing metrics and sharing insights. Collaborative reviews foster a sense of partnership and allow both parties to reflect on successes, challenges, and areas for improvement. This process ensures that influencers feel informed, appreciated, and motivated to optimize their content.

3. Celebrating Successes and Acknowledging Contributions

Celebrating milestones and achievements reinforces the partnership's value and makes influencers feel appreciated. Whether it's recognizing a successful campaign launch or reaching a specific sales target, acknowledging these accomplishments creates a positive experience for both parties. Brands might celebrate with social media shout-outs, bonuses, or even special events to thank influencers for their contributions.

4. Refining Future Campaigns Based on Insights

Analyzing campaign results provides valuable insights into audience preferences, engagement trends, and the effectiveness of different content formats. By refining future campaigns based on these insights, brands ensure that their influencer partnerships remain dynamic, impactful, and aligned with evolving audience expectations.

Conclusion: The Value of Building Strong Influencer Relationships

Building strong relationships with influencers is a cornerstone of effective influencer marketing. By focusing on transparency, trust, collaboration, and shared success, brands can create partnerships that go beyond surface-level endorsements to foster loyalty, authenticity, and long-term impact. These relationships, nurtured over time, enable influencers to become true advocates for the brand, driving genuine engagement and building lasting connections with audiences.

As we move into the next chapter, we'll explore how brands can create compelling, collaborative content with influencers that not only engages audiences but also aligns with campaign objectives, reinforcing the strength of the influencer-brand relationship and maximizing the partnership's impact.

Chapter 6: Creating Compelling, Collaborative Content

Introduction

In influencer marketing, content is at the heart of a campaign's success. Yet, simply producing content isn't enough; the content needs to resonate with audiences, align with both the influencer's and the brand's identities, and foster genuine connections. Collaborative content creation allows influencers to maintain their voice while authentically integrating the brand's message, resulting in compelling and relatable content that feels natural, not forced. This chapter dives into the art of creating content that engages, inspires, and drives results by leveraging the strengths of both the influencer and the brand.

From setting content objectives and brainstorming ideas to leveraging diverse formats and storytelling techniques, this chapter will guide brands in fostering a collaborative process that results in meaningful and impactful content.

Section 1: Setting Clear Content Objectives

Compelling content creation begins with clear, well-defined objectives that align with the campaign's broader goals. By setting content objectives from the outset, brands and influencers can craft a cohesive content strategy that drives engagement and achieves specific outcomes.

1. Defining Content Goals

Content goals should be specific and measurable, providing a clear direction for the campaign. Goals might include increasing brand awareness, driving engagement, promoting a new product, or educating the audience on a particular topic. For example, a beauty brand might focus on educating the audience about sustainable skincare practices, while a tech company may want to drive traffic to a new product launch.

It's essential to communicate these goals to the influencer early on, allowing them to tailor their content to support the campaign's objectives. Influencers who understand the content's purpose are better equipped to create impactful, focused messages that resonate with their audience.

2. Aligning Content Goals with Audience Needs

While setting content goals, brands should also consider the audience's needs and interests. Audiences respond best to content that is informative, entertaining, or inspiring, so aligning brand objectives with audience expectations ensures the content will be well-received. For instance, a fitness brand might aim to increase engagement by creating workout content with an influencer, appealing to followers' fitness interests while showcasing the brand's products.

By aligning content objectives with audience interests, brands create a foundation for content that feels relevant and valuable, increasing the chances of meaningful engagement and conversion.

3. Establishing Key Messages and Themes

To maintain coherence across the campaign, brands should define key messages and themes that will guide content creation. Key messages could include product benefits, brand values, or campaign slogans, while themes might revolve around specific lifestyle elements like sustainability, wellness, or adventure. These elements help create a narrative thread that runs through all campaign content, making it easy for the audience to understand and connect with the brand's message.

For example, a travel brand partnering with influencers might focus on themes of exploration, relaxation, or cultural discovery. By weaving these themes into the content, brands and influencers can create a unified story that captures the audience's attention and builds a consistent brand image.

Section 2: Brainstorming Collaborative Content Ideas

Collaboration is key to creating content that feels authentic and resonates with the influencer's audience. When brands and influencers brainstorm ideas together, they're able to merge the brand's messaging with the influencer's unique voice and perspective.

1. Conducting Joint Brainstorming Sessions

Joint brainstorming sessions provide an opportunity for brands and influencers to share ideas, align on creative concepts, and refine their approach. Brands might bring initial concepts, while influencers offer insights on what resonates with their followers. During these sessions, brands should encourage influencers to share their vision for the content, allowing for creative input that results in innovative and original ideas.

For instance, a lifestyle brand might present themes like "morning routines" or "self-care rituals," inviting the influencer to share how they would incorporate these themes authentically. This approach creates a sense of ownership for the influencer and ensures the content feels genuine to their audience.

2. Co-Creating Storylines and Narratives

Storytelling is one of the most powerful tools in influencer marketing, as it enables audiences to connect with content on a personal level. By co-creating storylines, brands and influencers can craft narratives that are both engaging and relatable. For example, rather than simply showcasing a product, an influencer might share a personal story about how the product has become part of their daily routine.

Brands can enhance storytelling by encouraging influencers to document their journey, show behind-the-scenes moments, or share personal insights. A fitness influencer, for example, could share a "day in the life" story, highlighting how the brand's products help them achieve their fitness goals, making the content more personal and relatable.

3. Creating Content Series for Consistency and Depth

A content series allows brands and influencers to explore topics in greater depth, creating a narrative that unfolds over time. Content series work particularly well for long-term partnerships, as they give followers multiple touchpoints to engage with the brand. For example, a food influencer collaborating with a cookware brand might create a weekly cooking series, with each episode showcasing a new recipe using the brand's products.

Content series are effective because they build anticipation and encourage followers to return for each installment, increasing engagement and fostering a deeper connection with the brand.

4. Involving the Audience in Content Creation

Inviting the audience to participate in content creation can increase engagement and make the campaign feel more interactive. Brands and influencers might encourage followers to share their experiences, answer polls, or submit questions for Q&A sessions. This level of involvement fosters a sense of community and makes the audience feel like an integral part of the campaign.

For example, a skincare brand working with an influencer might hold a Q&A session where followers can submit questions about skincare routines, allowing the influencer to address their concerns and offer personalized advice. Audience involvement creates a feedback loop that strengthens engagement and makes the content feel more dynamic and responsive.

Section 3: Experimenting with Diverse Content Formats

Different content formats allow brands and influencers to connect with audiences in varied and impactful ways. By experimenting with diverse formats, brands can reach different segments of the influencer's audience and maximize the campaign's impact.

1. Video Content for Storytelling and Demonstrations

Video content is one of the most engaging formats available, making it ideal for storytelling and product demonstrations. Platforms like Instagram, YouTube, and TikTok are optimized for video, providing influencers with the tools to create dynamic, visually appealing content. Brands might work with influencers on formats like tutorials, behind-the-scenes looks, or product unboxings, allowing audiences to see the product in action.

For instance, a beauty brand might collaborate with an influencer to create a skincare routine video, demonstrating how each product is used and its benefits. Video content enables followers to see the product in a real-world context, making it easier to visualize the brand's impact on their own lives.

2. Interactive Content for Enhanced Engagement

Interactive content formats, such as polls, quizzes, and Q&A sessions, offer a way for followers to actively participate in the campaign. These formats create a two-way interaction, increasing audience engagement and allowing brands to gain insights into audience preferences.

For example, a fashion influencer working with a clothing brand could create an Instagram Story poll where followers vote on different outfits, making them feel involved in the decision-making process. Interactive content fosters a sense of involvement, making followers feel more connected to both the influencer and the brand.

3. Short-Form Content for Quick Impact

Short-form content, like TikTok videos and Instagram Reels, is ideal for capturing attention quickly and delivering messages in a concise, impactful way. These formats are particularly effective for product teasers, trends, or humorous content, as they cater to short attention spans and encourage rapid engagement.

For example, a snack brand might work with influencers to create quick recipe videos featuring their products. Short-form content is easy to consume, shareable, and aligns with current social media trends, making it highly effective for building awareness and driving immediate engagement.

4. Blog Posts and Long-Form Content for In-Depth Information

While short-form content is effective for grabbing attention, long-form content, such as blog posts or YouTube videos, allows for in-depth storytelling and information sharing. Long-form content is particularly valuable for educational campaigns, product launches, or topics that require detailed explanations.

For example, a tech influencer collaborating with a gadget brand might create an in-depth YouTube review, discussing the product's features, benefits, and performance. This type of content helps build trust by providing followers with detailed information, making it especially valuable for high-consideration purchases.

Section 4: Ensuring Brand and Influencer Alignment in Content

To create content that feels authentic and coherent, brands and influencers must ensure their messaging, tone, and visuals are aligned. This alignment builds a unified brand story that resonates with audiences while allowing the influencer to retain their unique voice.

1. Crafting Brand Messaging that Feels Genuine

Brand messaging should be clear but flexible, allowing influencers to interpret it in a way that feels authentic to their audience. Forcing rigid scripts can make content feel unnatural, while allowing influencers to adapt key messages fosters authenticity. Brands should provide influencers with high-level messaging but encourage them to personalize it.

For instance, a wellness brand might communicate its commitment to mental health, allowing influencers to share their own mental wellness practices and how the brand's products support them. This approach maintains brand messaging while making it relevant to the influencer's personal journey.

2. Adapting Visuals to Fit the Influencer's Style

Visual consistency is essential for reinforcing brand identity, but it shouldn't compromise the influencer's aesthetic. Brands should provide visual guidelines, such as color schemes or mood boards, but leave room for the influencer's style. This balance allows the brand to stay visually recognizable while fitting naturally into the influencer's content.

For example, a luxury fashion brand might suggest a sophisticated, high-quality aesthetic but let the influencer style the clothing in a way that suits their personality. Visual alignment enhances brand recognition while maintaining authenticity and appeal.

3. Balancing Promotional Content with Organic Content

Content that feels overly promotional can disengage audiences, so it's crucial to strike a balance. Incorporating organic, non-promotional content into the campaign makes the partnership feel more genuine. Brands might consider a content mix that includes both promotional and lifestyle-focused content, allowing the influencer to naturally showcase the product's place in their life.

For instance, a beverage brand working with an influencer could encourage them to share lifestyle posts featuring the drink as part of a daily routine, rather than overtly focusing on product features. This subtle approach reinforces the brand's presence while keeping the content relatable.

4. Maintaining Consistency Across All Content

Consistency across all content formats reinforces brand messaging and fosters familiarity. Brands should collaborate with influencers to develop a cohesive content calendar, ensuring a consistent posting frequency and unified narrative. Consistency helps build trust, as audiences recognize the brand's presence in the influencer's life over time.

Section 5: Measuring Content Success and Learning from Insights

Measuring the success of collaborative content is essential to understanding what resonates with audiences and optimizing future campaigns. By analyzing performance metrics and gathering insights, brands can continually improve their content strategies.

1. Identifying Key Content Performance Metrics

Relevant metrics may include engagement rate, reach, impressions, click-through rate, and conversions. These metrics indicate how well the content resonates with the audience and whether it drives desired actions. For example, a high engagement rate on an interactive post suggests that followers are invested, while click-through rates reveal interest in exploring more about the brand.

2. Gathering Feedback from Influencers and Audiences

Feedback from both influencers and audiences can provide valuable insights into content effectiveness. Brands should encourage influencers to share their observations on what worked well and what didn't, while audience comments offer direct feedback. Audience responses help brands understand preferences and refine future content.

3. Analyzing Trends and Patterns

Identifying trends and patterns in content performance allows brands to make data-driven decisions. For instance, if videos consistently outperform static images, brands can focus on producing more video content in future campaigns. Trends provide actionable insights that inform content strategy adjustments.

4. Optimizing Future Campaigns Based on Insights

Content creation is an iterative process. By using insights from each campaign, brands can optimize future content strategies, improving alignment, engagement, and authenticity. Continual refinement strengthens influencer partnerships and ensures long-term success.

Conclusion: Creating Lasting Impact through Compelling Content

Creating compelling, collaborative content is both an art and a science. By setting clear objectives, fostering a collaborative environment, experimenting with diverse formats, ensuring alignment, and measuring performance, brands and influencers can create content that resonates with audiences on a deeper level. This collaborative approach fosters authenticity, builds trust, and maximizes the impact of influencer marketing campaigns.

As we move into the next chapter, we'll explore how brands can nurture these relationships over time, transforming one-off campaigns into long-term partnerships that yield enduring results and create lasting brand loyalty.

Chapter 7: Nurturing Long-Term Partnerships

Introduction

In influencer marketing, long-term partnerships provide a level of authenticity and impact that one-off campaigns often can't match. While short-term collaborations may deliver quick bursts of visibility, ongoing partnerships cultivate trust, deepen relationships, and allow influencers to integrate a brand authentically into their lives over time. These sustained collaborations turn influencers into brand advocates, building loyalty among their followers and reinforcing the brand's reputation.

In this chapter, we'll explore how brands can foster and nurture long-term relationships with influencers. From understanding the benefits of sustained partnerships to establishing mutual goals and navigating challenges, this chapter provides a roadmap for brands looking to build authentic, impactful, and enduring influencer relationships.

Section 1: The Benefits of Long-Term Influencer Partnerships

Long-term partnerships provide both brands and influencers with a range of benefits that can lead to increased trust, loyalty, and mutual growth.

1. Enhanced Trust and Authenticity

When influencers work with a brand repeatedly, their endorsements naturally feel more authentic. Followers notice when influencers integrate a brand into their lives over time, interpreting it as a genuine preference rather than a paid obligation. Repeated endorsements show audiences that the influencer truly values the brand, which increases trust and credibility.

For example, an influencer who consistently uses and discusses a skincare brand over several months demonstrates a genuine commitment to the product. This long-term connection makes followers more likely to trust the endorsement and consider the product for themselves.

2. Stronger Audience Engagement

Long-term partnerships often lead to higher audience engagement. When followers see a brand featured multiple times by the same influencer, they're more likely to recognize and remember it. Over time, audiences become familiar with the brand, which can lead to increased interest and curiosity. This familiarity encourages engagement, as followers may ask questions, seek advice, or even share their own experiences with the brand.

A fitness influencer, for instance, who regularly promotes a particular protein powder brand may receive questions from followers about the product's benefits, usage tips, and results, creating an ongoing dialogue around the brand.

3. Improved Brand Recall and Loyalty

Long-term partnerships build brand loyalty not only with the influencer but also with their followers. Repeated exposure to a brand increases recall, making it more likely that followers will remember the brand when making purchase decisions. Additionally, followers who see a brand consistently recommended by a trusted influencer are more likely to feel loyal to it.

Brands like Nike and Adidas, for example, maintain long-term relationships with athletes and fitness influencers. These partnerships are not just about individual campaigns; they're part of a larger strategy to foster loyalty and maintain brand association with high-performance sports and fitness.

4. Opportunities for Creative Collaboration and Growth

Long-term partnerships allow for deeper creative collaboration. Over time, influencers gain a more comprehensive understanding of the brand, enabling them to develop content that aligns closely with brand values. This ongoing relationship also gives both parties the opportunity to try new formats, test ideas, and innovate together, leading to campaigns that feel fresh and impactful.

For instance, a fashion brand working with an influencer season after season can develop more cohesive campaigns, incorporating new styles, trends, and collections that keep the content engaging and relevant.

Section 2: Building the Foundation for Long-Term Partnerships

Building a strong foundation for a long-term partnership requires intentional planning, clear communication, and shared values.

1. Identifying Mutual Goals and Values

The best long-term partnerships are built on a foundation of shared values. Before committing to an extended collaboration, brands should ensure that the influencer's values align with their own. Mutual goals are also crucial. Both the brand and the influencer should have a shared vision for the partnership, including objectives such as brand growth, audience education, or community building.

For example, an eco-conscious beauty brand looking for a long-term partnership should choose influencers who are genuinely passionate about sustainability. When both parties share a commitment to a cause, the content will feel authentic, and the partnership is more likely to succeed.

2. Setting Clear Expectations and Boundaries

Clear expectations help both the brand and the influencer understand their roles, responsibilities, and limitations within the partnership. This includes defining content requirements, timelines, compensation terms, and any exclusivity agreements. While flexibility is essential for creative freedom, setting clear boundaries ensures that both parties remain aligned throughout the partnership.

For instance, if a brand wants exclusivity within a product category, it's essential to discuss this upfront. A fitness brand, for example, might request that an influencer refrain from endorsing competing supplement brands for the duration of the partnership.

3. Creating a Formal Agreement

For long-term partnerships, it's advisable to create a formal contract that outlines the terms of the relationship. This agreement should cover key aspects such as deliverables, compensation, usage rights, confidentiality, and termination clauses. Contracts help prevent misunderstandings and provide a reference point if questions or challenges arise.

A well-structured agreement protects both the brand and the influencer, ensuring a smooth, professional relationship. Additionally, a contract gives influencers a sense of security, reinforcing their commitment to the partnership.

4. Regularly Evaluating the Partnership's Progress

Ongoing evaluation is crucial for ensuring that the partnership continues to meet both parties' expectations and objectives. Brands should schedule regular check-ins with influencers to discuss campaign performance, audience feedback, and potential areas for improvement. These conversations allow for adjustments, ensuring the partnership remains dynamic and responsive to changing trends.

For instance, a brand might conduct quarterly performance reviews with influencers to assess content impact, engagement rates, and follower sentiment. By analyzing these metrics, brands and influencers can refine their approach to maximize effectiveness.

Section 3: Cultivating Trust and Open Communication

Trust and open communication are the cornerstones of any successful long-term partnership. Without trust, influencers may feel constrained or undervalued, leading to content that feels forced rather than genuine.

1. Fostering Transparency and Honesty

Transparency is essential in a long-term partnership, as it encourages open dialogue and prevents misunderstandings. Brands should be upfront about their goals, values, and expectations, while influencers should feel comfortable sharing feedback, creative ideas, and concerns.

For example, if a brand is planning to launch a new product line, sharing this information with influencers in advance allows them to prepare relevant content ideas. Similarly, if an influencer is experiencing a personal challenge, they should feel comfortable communicating this to the brand, fostering an empathetic and understanding relationship.

2. Providing Consistent Support and Resources

Supporting influencers throughout the partnership ensures they feel valued and empowered. Brands should provide influencers with the resources they need to create high-quality content, including product samples, creative assets, and access to brand representatives for any questions. Regular support not only enhances content quality but also shows influencers that the brand is invested in their success.

For instance, a skincare brand might offer influencers training sessions on product ingredients and usage. This knowledge equips influencers to speak confidently about the products, resulting in more credible endorsements.

3. Encouraging Honest Feedback

Feedback is a two-way street in any successful partnership. Brands should provide constructive feedback on campaign performance, while influencers should feel comfortable sharing their thoughts on what's working and what isn't. This exchange of feedback promotes continuous improvement and strengthens the partnership.

For example, if an influencer finds that a particular content format resonates well with their audience, they can share this insight with the brand. Brands that welcome feedback are more likely to build loyal, invested influencer relationships, as influencers feel their contributions are genuinely valued.

4. Adapting to Changing Circumstances

Long-term partnerships should be flexible enough to adapt to changes, whether they're related to the influencer's personal life, shifts in audience preferences, or updates to the brand's goals.

Adapting to changing circumstances demonstrates empathy and helps the partnership remain relevant over time.

For instance, if an influencer's content focus shifts due to a lifestyle change, brands that accommodate this evolution may find new ways to collaborate, keeping the partnership fresh and aligned with the influencer's journey.

Section 4: Strategies for Sustaining Long-Term Partnerships

Maintaining a long-term partnership requires effort, creativity, and a commitment to keeping the collaboration engaging for both the influencer and their audience.

1. Innovating with New Content Formats

To keep the partnership exciting, brands and influencers should explore new content formats and styles. By introducing variety, they can prevent the content from feeling repetitive and capture audience interest. This might include experimenting with live streaming, short-form videos, or interactive content like Q&As and challenges.

For instance, a fashion brand working with an influencer over multiple seasons could try new formats, like behind-the-scenes looks at photo shoots, styling tips, or live shopping events. This variety keeps the audience engaged and invested in the brand's story.

2. Building Campaigns Around Personal Milestones

Personal milestones, such as birthdays, holidays, or major life events, offer unique opportunities for authentic brand-influencer content. Brands that acknowledge these milestones can create campaigns that feel personal and meaningful. Celebrating an influencer's birthday, for example, with a limited-edition product or customized gift set strengthens the partnership and enhances the brand's presence in their life.

A wellness brand, for instance, could support a fitness influencer's journey to a personal fitness goal, aligning the brand's message with the influencer's progress and achievements. These campaigns not only foster authenticity but also create memorable, emotionally resonant content.

3. Leveraging Influencer Insights for Brand Development

Influencers have valuable insights into audience preferences, content trends, and product feedback. By tapping into these insights, brands can make informed decisions about product development, marketing strategies, and customer service. Long-term influencer partnerships enable brands to gather ongoing feedback, adapting to changing consumer needs and staying relevant.

For example, a beauty brand working with influencers over time might gather feedback on product formulations, packaging, or shade ranges. This collaborative approach to product development fosters a sense of involvement and investment, as influencers feel they're contributing to the brand's growth.

4. Involving Influencers in Brand Initiatives and Events

Involving influencers in brand initiatives, such as product launches, charity events, or community programs, strengthens their connection to the brand. These initiatives allow influencers to become active participants in the brand's journey, creating content that goes beyond product promotion.

For example, a sustainable fashion brand might invite influencers to participate in a charity event promoting environmental awareness. This involvement creates shared experiences that deepen the influencer's commitment to the brand's mission and values.

Section 5: Measuring and Celebrating Success in Long-Term Partnerships

Celebrating achievements and measuring success is essential for maintaining momentum in long-term partnerships. Brands that recognize influencers' contributions foster loyalty and encourage ongoing engagement.

1. Defining Success Metrics for Long-Term Impact

In long-term partnerships, brands should establish metrics that reflect sustained impact rather than short-term gains. These metrics might include brand sentiment, loyalty, and follower retention, as well as conversion rates over time. By focusing on long-term metrics, brands can evaluate the partnership's effectiveness in building a loyal audience and driving lasting engagement.

2. Regularly Reviewing Performance and Setting New Goals

Performance reviews provide an opportunity for brands and influencers to reflect on the partnership's progress, celebrate successes, and set new goals. Brands should approach these reviews as collaborative discussions, where both parties can share insights and suggestions for improvement. Setting new goals keeps the partnership dynamic and forward-looking.

3. Celebrating Milestones and Recognizing Achievements

Celebrating achievements, whether they're related to sales targets, engagement milestones, or creative successes, reinforces the value of the partnership. Recognizing these accomplishments can include bonuses, personalized gifts, or social media shout-outs, demonstrating appreciation for the influencer's contributions.

For instance, a brand reaching its highest sales month due to an influencer-led campaign might send the influencer a personalized thank-you package, acknowledging their role in the success. These gestures build goodwill and make influencers feel genuinely appreciated.

4. Adapting and Optimizing Based on Insights

Continual adaptation is essential to sustaining a long-term partnership. By analyzing data, identifying successful content formats, and learning from audience feedback, brands can refine their approach to maximize impact. This iterative process ensures the partnership remains effective, responsive, and aligned with changing trends.

Conclusion: Building Enduring, Impactful Relationships

Long-term partnerships between brands and influencers offer a unique opportunity to foster authenticity, trust, and loyalty. By focusing on shared values, open communication, flexibility, and continuous adaptation, brands can create relationships that go beyond transactional endorsements. These sustained partnerships enable influencers to become true brand advocates, resonating deeply with their audience and creating lasting impact.

As brands embrace the power of long-term influencer relationships, they can drive growth, build community, and achieve sustainable success. In the next chapter, we'll explore strategies for measuring success beyond traditional metrics, ensuring that these partnerships yield both immediate and long-term benefits for both the brand and the influencer.

Chapter 8: Measuring Success Beyond Likes and Shares

Introduction

In influencer marketing, measuring success is critical—but in an evolving landscape, success goes beyond just likes, shares, and follower counts. To truly understand the impact of influencer campaigns, brands must adopt a holistic approach to performance measurement, looking at metrics that reflect long-term influence, brand loyalty, and audience sentiment. This chapter will guide you through advanced strategies for measuring the effectiveness of influencer partnerships, from defining relevant key performance indicators (KPIs) to leveraging data for continuous improvement.

As we'll explore in this chapter, tracking deeper metrics—such as brand sentiment, conversion rates, and audience loyalty—allows brands to assess their campaigns' real impact and make data-driven decisions that enhance future partnerships. This chapter will provide tools, techniques, and best practices for tracking and interpreting these essential metrics, ensuring brands maximize the value of their influencer relationships.

Section 1: Establishing Relevant KPIs for Long-Term Impact

Setting KPIs tailored to long-term objectives is the foundation of effective influencer campaign measurement. These KPIs should go beyond short-term indicators like impressions or engagement to capture broader goals, such as audience loyalty, brand perception, and customer lifetime value.

1. Aligning KPIs with Campaign Goals

The first step in setting meaningful KPIs is to align them with the campaign's goals. For example, if a campaign's primary goal is to increase brand awareness, reach and share-of-voice metrics may be appropriate. Conversely, if the focus is on driving conversions, KPIs such as click-through rates, sales, and customer acquisition cost will be more relevant.

Common KPIs for Influencer Campaigns:

- **Brand Awareness KPIs**: Reach, impressions, share of voice, new followers.
- **Engagement KPIs**: Likes, comments, shares, engagement rate.
- **Conversion KPIs**: Click-through rate (CTR), conversion rate, cost per conversion, sales.
- **Brand Loyalty KPIs**: Repeat purchase rate, customer retention, customer lifetime value.
- **Brand Sentiment KPIs**: Sentiment analysis, net promoter score (NPS).

2. Incorporating Long-Term KPIs

While short-term metrics provide immediate feedback, long-term KPIs track ongoing impact, enabling brands to gauge sustained influence. For example, tracking repeat purchase rates or customer lifetime value (CLV) gives brands insight into the loyalty and financial impact of influencer campaigns over time. Long-term KPIs help brands assess whether influencer partnerships are building lasting connections with their audience.

Examples of Long-Term KPIs:

- **Customer Retention Rate**: Measures how well the influencer campaign fosters brand loyalty.
- **Customer Lifetime Value (CLV)**: Assesses the long-term revenue generated by customers acquired through influencer campaigns.
- **Brand Sentiment and Reputation**: Tracks how the audience's perception of the brand changes over time.

By focusing on both short- and long-term KPIs, brands can comprehensively assess their influencer campaigns' effectiveness and gain insights into how well these partnerships contribute to sustainable growth.

Section 2: Tracking Engagement and Brand Sentiment

Engagement and brand sentiment are critical indicators of an influencer campaign's success. While likes, comments, and shares are standard engagement metrics, understanding the quality of these interactions and how the audience feels about the brand is key to measuring true influence.

1. Analyzing Engagement Quality

Not all engagement is created equal. High-quality engagement reflects meaningful interactions that demonstrate genuine interest in the brand. Brands should analyze comments, shares, and direct messages to assess engagement quality. For example, detailed comments with questions or feedback suggest a more invested audience than simple emoji reactions.

Quality Engagement Indicators:

- **Comments that ask questions**: Indicates genuine interest and curiosity about the product or brand.
- **Shares and reposts**: Demonstrates endorsement, as followers find the content valuable enough to share.
- **Meaningful interactions**: Conversations or feedback that indicate deeper interest in the brand.

High-quality engagement shows that followers aren't just passively consuming content but are actively engaged, increasing the likelihood of brand loyalty and conversion.

2. Leveraging Sentiment Analysis

Sentiment analysis examines the tone and emotion behind audience interactions, revealing how followers feel about the brand. Brands can use social listening tools to analyze sentiment across comments, direct messages, and social media mentions, enabling them to gauge the campaign's impact on brand perception.

Positive sentiment suggests that followers have a favorable view of the brand, while negative sentiment may indicate dissatisfaction or skepticism. By regularly tracking sentiment, brands can understand how influencer campaigns influence brand perception and make adjustments as needed.

3. Monitoring Brand Advocacy

Brand advocacy is a powerful metric in influencer marketing. Loyal followers who actively recommend the brand to others are invaluable, as they can drive organic growth. Brands can track advocacy by monitoring brand mentions, hashtag usage, and user-generated content (UGC) inspired by the influencer campaign. For instance, if followers begin sharing their own experiences with the brand after an influencer's post, it indicates that the influencer's endorsement is resonating on a deeper level.

Section 3: Measuring Conversions and ROI

While engagement and sentiment are valuable metrics, conversions and ROI provide a clear picture of the campaign's financial impact. Tracking conversions shows how influencer campaigns directly contribute to revenue, while ROI helps brands understand the cost-effectiveness of their influencer partnerships.

1. Tracking Conversion Metrics

Conversion metrics reveal how well an influencer campaign drives tangible actions, such as sales, sign-ups, or downloads. Brands can measure conversions through unique links, promo codes, or tracking pixels embedded in influencer content.

Key Conversion Metrics:

- **Click-Through Rate (CTR)**: Measures the percentage of followers who clicked on a link within the influencer's content.
- **Conversion Rate**: The percentage of clicks that led to the desired action, such as a purchase or sign-up.

- **Cost Per Conversion**: The cost of each conversion, helping brands assess the cost-effectiveness of the campaign.

These metrics provide insight into the campaign's ability to generate interest and drive actions that align with business goals.

2. ROI

Return on investment (ROI) is a critical metric in influencer marketing, as it assesses the financial value of the campaign. Calculating ROI involves comparing the campaign's revenue to its total costs, including influencer fees, production costs, and any additional marketing expenses. ROI helps brands determine whether the influencer partnership is profitable, guiding future budget allocation.

3. Evaluating Customer Lifetime Value (CLV) from Influencer Acquisitions

Beyond immediate conversions, customer lifetime value (CLV) measures the long-term financial contribution of customers acquired through influencer campaigns. If an influencer attracts high-value customers who make repeat purchases, the campaign's true ROI is much higher. Tracking CLV provides a more comprehensive understanding of how influencer partnerships contribute to brand growth over time.

For instance, if a beauty influencer attracts customers who spend an average of $200 per year on a skincare brand's products, the long-term ROI of this partnership may justify higher initial investment.

Section 4: Using Advanced Analytics Tools for Influencer Campaigns

Various tools and platforms can streamline performance tracking, helping brands measure influencer campaigns effectively and gain insights to guide future decisions.

1. Social Media Analytics Platforms

Most social media platforms offer built-in analytics tools for tracking basic metrics, such as reach, impressions, and engagement. Platforms like Instagram, Facebook, and YouTube provide insights into follower demographics, engagement rates, and post performance. Brands can leverage these tools to monitor campaign effectiveness in real-time and make data-driven adjustments.

For example, Instagram Insights provides data on post reach, saves, shares, and interactions, enabling brands to track which posts resonate best with followers. YouTube Analytics, meanwhile, provides detailed viewer demographics, watch time, and audience retention, helping brands understand how long users are engaging with video content.

2. Third-Party Analytics Tools

Third-party analytics tools like Sprout Social, Hootsuite, and Brandwatch offer advanced features for monitoring engagement, sentiment, and audience demographics across multiple platforms. These tools can aggregate data, providing a holistic view of campaign performance and enabling brands to track influencer impact beyond individual platforms.

Many of these tools also include social listening capabilities, allowing brands to monitor brand mentions, track sentiment trends, and identify brand advocates. Social listening provides valuable insights into how the audience perceives the brand, even outside the influencer's direct content.

3. Affiliate and Conversion Tracking Platforms

For campaigns focused on conversions, affiliate and conversion tracking platforms, such as Google Analytics, Refersion, and Impact, help brands track clicks, conversions, and revenue generated by influencers. Brands can assign unique links or discount codes to each influencer, providing a clear attribution path for conversions.

These platforms enable brands to measure conversion rates, track customer journeys, and attribute revenue to specific influencers, allowing for accurate ROI assessment.

4. Sentiment Analysis Tools

Sentiment analysis tools, like Talkwalker and NetBase, use AI to interpret the tone and emotion behind social media comments, mentions, and posts. By analyzing audience sentiment, brands can understand how influencer campaigns impact brand perception and identify any potential issues early.

For example, if sentiment analysis reveals a spike in positive comments following a campaign, it suggests that the influencer's content resonated well with the audience. Conversely, a spike in negative sentiment may indicate issues that need to be addressed.

Section 5: Learning from Data to Optimize Future Campaigns

Data is only valuable if it's used to inform future decisions. By analyzing performance metrics and learning from campaign results, brands can continually refine their influencer strategies for greater impact.

1. Identifying Patterns and Trends

Patterns and trends in campaign performance offer insights into what resonates best with audiences. Brands should review past campaigns to identify successful content formats, messaging, and influencer types. For instance, if data consistently shows higher engagement rates for video content, brands can prioritize video in future campaigns.

2. Testing and Experimenting with Different Approaches

Experimentation is key to optimization. Brands should test various content types, messaging, and timing strategies to see what drives the most engagement, conversions, and sentiment. A/B testing, for example, can reveal which approach is more effective, providing data to guide future campaign decisions.

3. Applying Feedback from Influencers and Audiences

Both influencers and audiences provide valuable feedback that can shape future campaigns. Brands should encourage influencers to share their observations, as they have firsthand knowledge of what resonates with their followers. Similarly, audience feedback in the form of comments, surveys, or direct messages can reveal preferences and inform adjustments.

4. Refining Audience Targeting

Influencer campaigns provide insights into audience demographics, interests, and behavior. By analyzing this data, brands can refine their targeting strategies, ensuring that future campaigns reach the most relevant and receptive audience segments.

For example, if data shows that a campaign resonates particularly well with followers aged 18-24, brands can target similar demographics in future campaigns to maximize impact.

Conclusion: Measuring Success for Sustainable Growth

Measuring influencer campaign success goes beyond tracking likes and shares. By focusing on metrics that reflect long-term impact—such as brand loyalty, sentiment, and conversions—brands can assess the true effectiveness of their influencer partnerships. This data-driven approach allows brands to make informed decisions, optimize campaigns, and build sustainable relationships that yield lasting value.

By establishing relevant KPIs, using advanced analytics tools, and learning from each campaign, brands can refine their influencer strategies for greater effectiveness. In the final chapter, we'll explore emerging trends in influencer marketing, equipping brands to adapt to changes and stay at the forefront of this dynamic field.

Chapter 9: Emerging Trends in Authentic Influencer Marketing

Introduction

Influencer marketing is a dynamic field, constantly evolving as platforms, technologies, and consumer expectations shift. To remain competitive and relevant, brands need to stay informed of emerging trends that are reshaping the influencer landscape. As audiences become more discerning and saturated with content, influencers and brands are finding new ways to connect, create, and engage authentically. This chapter will explore key trends in influencer marketing, from the rise of niche micro-influencers and virtual influencers to the growing demand for socially responsible partnerships and interactive content.

By understanding these trends, brands can position themselves at the forefront of influencer marketing, capitalizing on new opportunities to build meaningful, impactful relationships with their audiences.

Section 1: The Rise of Niche and Micro-Influencers

Over the past few years, the influencer landscape has seen a significant shift from macro and mega influencers to micro and nano influencers. As audiences increasingly seek authentic connections, niche and micro-influencers have become more valuable due to their specialized knowledge, relatable personalities, and loyal, engaged communities.

1. Why Niche Influencers Are Gaining Popularity

Niche influencers are particularly effective because they serve well-defined communities with specific interests. They may focus on particular areas such as sustainable fashion, veganism, tech reviews, or mental health advocacy, which allows them to connect deeply with followers who share those passions. For brands, working with niche influencers can mean reaching an audience that is more receptive and likely to engage with the content, as it speaks directly to their interests and values.

For example, a sustainable skincare brand might partner with a niche influencer focused on zero-waste living, gaining access to a community that values sustainability and is more likely to purchase eco-friendly products.

2. Advantages of Micro and Nano Influencers

Micro influencers (10,000–100,000 followers) and nano influencers (fewer than 10,000 followers) typically have higher engagement rates than larger influencers, as they cultivate close-knit relationships with their audience. These smaller influencers are perceived as more relatable and accessible, which fosters trust and credibility. Followers often feel that they "know" these influencers personally, making their recommendations feel like advice from a friend rather than an advertisement.

Brands working with micro and nano influencers benefit from authentic connections, high-quality engagement, and often lower costs than those associated with larger influencers. This makes them ideal partners for small to medium-sized businesses or brands aiming for highly targeted campaigns.

3. Leveraging Local and Community-Centric Influencers

Local influencers, who operate within a specific geographic region, are another growing trend. Brands looking to drive foot traffic to physical stores, promote local events, or engage with community-based audiences are increasingly turning to these influencers. For example, a restaurant or fitness studio might partner with local influencers to attract nearby residents, achieving a more localized and relevant reach.

By tapping into niche, micro, and local influencers, brands can enhance the authenticity of their campaigns, reaching audiences in a way that feels personal and community-centered.

Section 2: Emphasis on Social Responsibility and Purpose-Driven Campaigns

Today's consumers expect brands to stand for something beyond profit, and influencer marketing is no exception. Audiences increasingly favor brands and influencers who support social, environmental, and ethical causes. In response, purpose-driven campaigns and socially responsible partnerships have become essential components of effective influencer marketing.

1. The Growing Demand for Social Responsibility

As issues like climate change, racial justice, and mental health awareness gain prominence, consumers are actively seeking brands that take a stand on these topics. Influencers who advocate for causes they care about resonate with followers who share their values. This alignment of values helps create a sense of community, as followers feel they are supporting not just a brand but a movement.

For example, an influencer who regularly discusses mental health and self-care might partner with a wellness brand that donates a portion of profits to mental health organizations. This partnership feels more meaningful to the influencer's audience, as they know their purchase contributes to a cause they care about.

2. Authentic Activism and Avoiding "Woke-Washing"

While aligning with social causes can be impactful, it must be done authentically. Audiences are quick to spot insincerity, and "woke-washing"—the practice of superficially supporting a cause for marketing purposes without meaningful action— can lead to backlash. Brands should ensure that their commitment to a cause is genuine and backed by real actions, such as charitable donations, sustainable practices, or corporate policies that support the cause.

Influencers are also scrutinized for authenticity when discussing social issues. Brands that partner with influencers who have a long-standing commitment to a cause are more likely to create an authentic, impactful campaign. For instance, a sustainable fashion brand partnering with an influencer who has advocated for eco-friendly practices for years would likely be viewed more favorably than a similar campaign launched solely for marketing purposes.

3. Purpose-Driven Storytelling

Purpose-driven campaigns benefit from storytelling that highlights the brand's values and mission. Influencers can share personal stories, experiences, or challenges related to the cause, creating an emotional connection with their audience. For example, a beauty influencer with a history of discussing skin conditions might partner with a skincare brand to discuss the challenges of sensitive skin, while also promoting a message of self-acceptance.

By incorporating storytelling into purpose-driven campaigns, brands can create content that goes beyond product promotion to inspire, educate, and build community around shared values.

Section 3: The Integration of Virtual and AI-Driven Influencers

With advancements in technology, virtual and AI-driven influencers are emerging as a unique category within influencer marketing. These digital personas, often created by brands or tech companies, provide a new way to connect with audiences in an imaginative, futuristic format.

1. What Are Virtual Influencers?

Virtual influencers are digital characters, often designed to look like real people, who exist exclusively on social media platforms. Unlike traditional influencers, virtual influencers are controlled by teams of designers, marketers, and writers, allowing for consistent brand messaging and control. These digital personas can create and share content, interact with followers, and even collaborate with brands.

Notable virtual influencers include Lil Miquela, a computer-generated character who shares lifestyle, fashion, and social justice content, and has partnered with major brands such as Calvin Klein and Prada.

2. The Appeal of Virtual Influencers for Brands

Virtual influencers offer several advantages. They are always on-brand, never age, and don't experience the personal challenges that can affect real influencers. They are highly customizable and can be adjusted to align with the brand's evolving goals or aesthetics. Virtual influencers also appeal to tech-savvy audiences, particularly among younger generations who value innovation and creativity.

However, brands must carefully consider their audience's response to virtual influencers. While some followers are intrigued by the novelty, others may find them impersonal or inauthentic. Virtual influencers are best suited for brands that prioritize innovation, such as fashion, gaming, and technology companies.

3. Ethical Considerations and Limitations of Virtual Influencers

The use of virtual influencers raises ethical questions around transparency and authenticity. Brands must be transparent about the fact that these characters are not real, as misleading audiences can lead to trust issues. Additionally, virtual influencers may lack the genuine relatability of real influencers, which can limit their appeal in campaigns that require emotional connection.

For example, a virtual influencer may be effective for promoting a tech gadget, but less so for a wellness product that relies on personal stories and authenticity. By carefully considering these limitations, brands can use virtual influencers as a complement to traditional influencer campaigns, rather than a replacement.

Section 4: The Power of Interactive and Experiential Content

As social media platforms introduce new features and audiences become more accustomed to engaging with content in dynamic ways, interactive and experiential content has become increasingly popular. This trend allows audiences to actively participate in campaigns, making the experience more memorable and impactful.

1. Interactive Content Formats

Interactive content formats, such as polls, quizzes, and live Q&A sessions, enable followers to engage directly with influencers and brands. This level of interaction fosters a sense of connection and makes the campaign feel more personalized. For example, an influencer could host a live Q&A session about a brand's skincare line, allowing followers to ask questions in real-time.

Brands can leverage interactive features like Instagram Stories' "Ask Me Anything" or TikTok's duet feature to engage followers and gather valuable feedback. By involving the audience, brands create a two-way conversation, which fosters stronger relationships and drives engagement.

2. The Rise of AR and VR Experiences

Augmented reality (AR) and virtual reality (VR) are transforming how brands and influencers create immersive, experiential content. AR filters on platforms like Instagram and Snapchat allow followers to virtually "try on" products, such as sunglasses or makeup. These features make the experience more engaging, allowing audiences to interact with the brand in a way that feels tangible and personalized.

For instance, a beauty brand could develop an AR filter that lets users try different lipstick shades, while an outdoor gear company could create a VR experience that simulates an adventure using their products. AR and VR experiences not only capture attention but also provide valuable insights into consumer preferences.

3. Gamification in Influencer Campaigns

Gamification, or incorporating game-like elements into content, adds an element of fun and competition to campaigns. Influencers can create challenges, contests, or interactive "missions" for their followers, encouraging participation and engagement. For example, a fitness influencer might create a 30-day fitness challenge in collaboration with a sportswear brand, with followers encouraged to share their progress.

Gamification is effective because it taps into intrinsic motivations like achievement, competition, and community. By incorporating game elements, brands can create memorable experiences that foster brand loyalty and encourage long-term engagement.

Section 5: Embracing Long-Form and Educational Content

While short-form content remains popular, there is a growing trend toward long-form, educational content as audiences seek deeper, more informative content from influencers. Platforms like YouTube, blogs, and even IGTV provide a space for influencers to dive into topics in depth, building credibility and trust with their followers.

1. The Appeal of Long-Form Content for In-Depth Storytelling

Long-form content enables influencers to tell stories, share insights, and connect with their audience on a deeper level. This format is especially effective for high-consideration products, such as technology, beauty, or wellness products, where audiences need detailed information before making a purchase.

For example, a tech influencer might produce an in-depth YouTube review of a new gadget, covering its features, pros and cons, and performance. This type of content provides value to followers, helping them make informed decisions and increasing the brand's credibility.

2. Educational Content as a Value-Add

Educational content is highly effective for brands aiming to position themselves as experts in their industry. Influencers can create tutorials, how-to guides, or informational posts that provide followers with practical knowledge. For example, a nutrition brand might partner with a wellness influencer to share recipes, meal plans, or nutritional tips.

This type of content builds trust, as followers see the brand as a source of valuable information rather than just a product provider. By focusing on education, brands can foster loyalty, encouraging followers to view the brand as a long-term resource.

3. The Popularity of Podcasting and Audio Content

Podcasting is a growing format within influencer marketing, particularly for brands and influencers looking to discuss complex topics, share personal stories, or connect in an intimate, conversational format. Brands can sponsor episodes, create branded podcasts, or appear as guests on influencers' shows to reach a targeted, engaged audience.

For example, a mental health app might collaborate with a wellness influencer who hosts a podcast, where they discuss topics like mindfulness, self-care, and mental health tips. Audio content allows for deeper exploration and is convenient for audiences to consume on the go, making it a valuable addition to long-form influencer strategies.

Conclusion: Staying Ahead in Influencer Marketing

As the influencer marketing landscape continues to evolve, brands that stay informed of emerging trends can capitalize on new opportunities to connect with audiences in authentic, impactful ways. From leveraging niche and micro-influencers to embracing virtual influencers, interactive content, and purpose-driven campaigns, these trends reflect a shift toward deeper, more meaningful engagement.

By understanding and integrating these trends, brands can craft influencer campaigns that resonate with today's consumers, fostering trust, loyalty, and lasting connections. As we move to the final chapter, we'll explore how brands can prepare for the future of influencer marketing, ensuring they remain adaptable and resilient in this fast-changing industry.

Chapter 10: Preparing for the Future of Influencer Marketing

Introduction

Influencer marketing has grown exponentially over the last decade, becoming one of the most effective ways for brands to connect with consumers. However, the influencer landscape is evolving rapidly, influenced by changes in technology, social media trends, consumer preferences, and regulations. To stay relevant and resilient, brands must not only embrace current trends but also proactively prepare for what lies ahead. This final chapter will explore strategies that brands can implement to future-proof their influencer marketing efforts, from staying adaptable and prioritizing authenticity to leveraging new technologies and complying with regulatory guidelines.

By understanding and planning for the future of influencer marketing, brands can position themselves to thrive in an ever-changing environment. This chapter will provide actionable steps to help brands navigate the shifting landscape and create influencer marketing strategies that stand the test of time.

Section 1: Embracing Agility and Adaptability in Influencer Marketing

One of the most crucial qualities for brands in the future of influencer marketing is adaptability. Social media platforms, audience preferences, and influencer dynamics are constantly changing, and brands that can pivot quickly are more likely to succeed.

1. Staying Updated on Platform Changes and Trends

Social media platforms frequently introduce new features, algorithms, and content formats. For example, Instagram introduced Reels to compete with TikTok, and LinkedIn introduced Creator Mode to encourage influencer-style content on its platform. Brands that stay updated on these changes can be early adopters, leveraging new features to capture attention and remain relevant.

Brands should establish processes to regularly monitor changes on key platforms, either through dedicated social media managers or agency partners. This could include subscribing to industry news sources, attending social media conferences, or following updates directly from platform announcements. Staying informed allows brands to adapt their strategies and make the most of new tools and trends.

2. Developing an Agile Influencer Strategy

An agile influencer strategy means being open to experimenting, analyzing results, and making quick adjustments based on data. Instead of committing to long-term plans that don't allow flexibility, brands should adopt a test-and-learn approach. This can include experimenting with different types of influencers (e.g., micro vs. macro), content formats (e.g., video vs. image), and campaign structures (e.g., one-off vs. long-term partnerships).

For example, a beauty brand might run several short-term campaigns with different influencers, testing which approaches and audiences are most effective before committing to a larger, more comprehensive campaign. This approach allows brands to respond to what's working in real-time and allocate resources more effectively.

3. Building a Diverse Influencer Portfolio

To future-proof influencer marketing efforts, brands should build a diverse influencer portfolio. Relying on a single type of influencer or a small group can be risky if trends or consumer preferences shift. Instead, brands should work with a mix of macro, micro, nano, and even virtual influencers to reach a wide array of audiences.

A diverse influencer portfolio allows brands to target different demographics and experiment with various content types, increasing resilience in case one segment becomes less effective. For instance, a fitness brand might partner with a macro influencer for widespread reach, micro influencers for niche appeal, and a virtual influencer for tech-savvy audiences, creating a multi-dimensional approach to reach different consumer segments.

Section 2: Prioritizing Transparency and Authenticity

As consumers become increasingly aware of and critical of marketing tactics, transparency and authenticity have never been more important. The future of influencer marketing relies heavily on the brand's ability to maintain credibility and trust.

1. Disclosing Sponsored Content

Transparency is critical to maintaining audience trust, and disclosing sponsored content is a crucial aspect of this transparency. In recent years, regulatory bodies like the Federal Trade Commission (FTC) in the United States have introduced stricter guidelines requiring influencers to clearly disclose partnerships. These disclosures help consumers make informed decisions and preserve the integrity of the influencer-brand relationship.

Brands should ensure that all influencer partners understand and comply with disclosure requirements, using clear language such as #ad or

#sponsored in captions. Educating influencers on these guidelines and consistently reinforcing them shows a commitment to ethical marketing, which resonates positively with audiences.

2. Encouraging Authentic Storytelling

To remain effective, influencer content must feel genuine and not overly promotional. Brands should encourage influencers to tell authentic stories that naturally integrate the product or service into their lives. This approach feels less like a sales pitch and more like a personal recommendation, which builds trust and makes followers more likely to engage with the content.

For example, instead of requiring a skincare influencer to use a pre-written caption, a brand could ask them to share their genuine experiences with the product and explain how it fits into their daily routine. Giving influencers the freedom to personalize their messaging leads to more authentic content that resonates deeply with audiences.

3. Partnering with Value-Aligned Influencers

The future of influencer marketing will see consumers placing more importance on the values and ethics of both brands and influencers. As a result, brands must be selective about whom they partner with, choosing influencers whose values align with their own. Consumers expect influencers to represent brands they genuinely believe in, and any disconnect between influencer and brand values can lead to skepticism or backlash.

For instance, a sustainable fashion brand should prioritize working with influencers who advocate for environmental responsibility and are known for promoting eco-friendly practices. Partnering with value-aligned influencers ensures authenticity and makes campaigns more credible, especially as consumers become increasingly values-driven.

Section 3: Leveraging Emerging Technologies in Influencer Marketing

Technology is revolutionizing influencer marketing, offering new ways to engage audiences, track performance, and optimize campaigns. Brands that embrace emerging technologies can stay ahead of the curve and create more impactful, data-driven strategies.

1. AI and Machine Learning for Audience Insights

Artificial intelligence (AI) and machine learning are transforming how brands understand audience preferences and behaviors. By analyzing vast amounts of data, AI-powered tools can provide insights into audience demographics, sentiment, engagement patterns, and content preferences, allowing brands to select influencers who align closely with their target audience.

For instance, AI can help brands predict which influencers are most likely to drive conversions based on previous campaign data. It can also suggest the best times to post, the ideal content format, and even the language that resonates best with specific demographics. By leveraging AI, brands can make more informed decisions and create tailored, effective influencer campaigns.

2. The Impact of Augmented Reality (AR) and Virtual Reality (VR)

Augmented reality (AR) and virtual reality (VR) are creating immersive experiences that can elevate influencer campaigns. AR filters on Instagram and Snapchat allow users to virtually "try on" products, making it easier for consumers to visualize how a product fits into their lives. Similarly, VR experiences enable users to engage with a brand in a fully immersive environment, such as exploring a virtual store or trying out a new product feature.

Brands can partner with influencers to create custom AR filters or VR experiences that their followers can engage with directly. For instance, a makeup brand could design an AR filter that allows users to try different lipstick shades, which the influencer promotes in a tutorial. These interactive experiences enhance engagement and make influencer content more memorable.

3. Blockchain and Transparency in Influencer Marketing

Blockchain technology, primarily known for its role in cryptocurrency, is being explored as a tool to bring greater transparency and accountability to influencer marketing. By recording and verifying interactions on an immutable ledger, blockchain can provide an additional layer of transparency, reducing fraudulent activities like fake engagement and bots.

For example, blockchain can be used to verify follower authenticity and engagement metrics, ensuring that brands are investing in influencers with real, engaged audiences. This technology could also facilitate clearer tracking of contract terms and deliverables, enhancing trust and transparency in influencer partnerships.

Section 4: Navigating Evolving Regulations and Compliance

As influencer marketing matures, regulatory bodies worldwide are establishing guidelines to ensure ethical practices. Compliance with these regulations is essential for maintaining credibility, avoiding legal issues, and upholding audience trust.

1. Understanding Global Disclosure Requirements

Disclosure requirements vary by country, with some regions enforcing stricter guidelines than others. For example, the FTC in the U.S., the Advertising Standards Authority (ASA) in the U.K., and similar bodies in other countries require clear and conspicuous disclosure of paid partnerships. These requirements are in place to prevent deceptive marketing practices and ensure that consumers can easily identify sponsored content.

Brands that work with influencers across multiple countries must be aware of these differing regulations and ensure that all partnerships comply with the relevant standards. Establishing clear disclosure guidelines within influencer contracts and providing education on compliance requirements helps maintain transparency and avoid regulatory issues.

2. Monitoring for Compliance with Brand Safety Standards

Brand safety has become a top priority as brands seek to protect their reputation in a highly public digital environment. Influencer marketing campaigns must align with brand safety standards, ensuring that influencers do not share controversial or offensive content that could negatively impact the brand's image.

Brands can implement brand safety protocols by thoroughly vetting influencers, using tools to monitor influencer content, and establishing contract clauses that outline acceptable behavior. Maintaining open communication with influencers also helps ensure that they understand and respect the brand's values, fostering a partnership built on mutual respect and shared standards.

3. Preparing for Data Privacy Regulations

Data privacy regulations, such as the General Data Protection Regulation (GDPR) in the EU, impact how brands and influencers collect, store, and use consumer data. These regulations require brands to be transparent about data collection practices, secure personal information, and obtain consent when necessary.

For example, if an influencer campaign includes collecting consumer information through sign-ups or surveys, brands must ensure that data privacy practices comply with relevant regulations. Partnering with legal experts or compliance professionals can help brands navigate these requirements, protecting consumer privacy and building trust.

Section 5: Creating a Resilient, Long-Term Influencer Marketing Strategy

Future-proofing influencer marketing involves building a strategy that's adaptable, sustainable, and capable of delivering long-term value. Rather than relying solely on short-term gains, brands should focus on creating relationships and campaigns that yield ongoing benefits.

1. Building Relationships with Influencers as Long-Term Partners

In the future, the most successful influencer campaigns will be those rooted in genuine, long-term partnerships. By fostering deep relationships with influencers, brands can create advocates who represent the brand consistently and credibly. Long-term partnerships lead to more authentic content, as influencers genuinely incorporate the brand into their lives.

For instance, a wellness brand might work with a health influencer over the course of a year, allowing the influencer to document their journey with the product. This approach provides the audience with a deeper understanding of the brand's impact and builds credibility through sustained engagement.

2. Prioritizing Value-Driven Content Over Promotional Content

Future audiences are likely to be even more selective, favoring content that provides value over content that feels purely promotional. Brands should prioritize value-driven content that educates, inspires, or entertains the audience. This can include tutorials, how-to guides, behind-the-scenes content, and other formats that focus on storytelling rather than direct promotion.

For example, a food brand could partner with a chef influencer to create educational content about healthy meal prep, positioning the brand as a helpful resource rather than simply a product provider. By offering value, brands can build trust and encourage followers to engage more meaningfully.

3. Measuring Success Beyond Vanity Metrics

As influencer marketing matures, brands should move beyond vanity metrics like likes and views, focusing instead on metrics that reflect long-term impact. Metrics such as customer retention, lifetime value, and brand sentiment provide a more accurate picture of campaign effectiveness and brand loyalty.

By investing in tools and techniques that track these deeper metrics, brands can gain insights into what drives genuine engagement and make data-driven decisions that strengthen their influencer strategies.

Conclusion: Shaping the Future of Influencer Marketing

The future of influencer marketing will be defined by adaptability, authenticity, and a commitment to ethical practices. As platforms, technologies, and regulations continue to evolve, brands that proactively embrace these changes will remain resilient and relevant. By focusing on transparency, leveraging emerging technologies, complying with regulations, and creating value-driven, long-term partnerships, brands can build sustainable influencer marketing strategies that resonate with audiences for years to come.

Preparing for the future requires continuous learning, flexibility, and a commitment to authenticity. By staying ahead of industry shifts and maintaining a people-first approach, brands can continue to harness the power of influencer marketing to foster meaningful connections, inspire audiences, and drive lasting impact.

Chapter 11: Future-Proofing Your Brand's Influencer Marketing Strategy

Introduction

As influencer marketing continues to evolve, brands need to build strategies that are not only effective today but also resilient to future changes. A future-proof influencer marketing strategy combines adaptability, innovation, and a focus on long-term relationships, ensuring that brands can thrive despite industry shifts, emerging technologies, or changing consumer expectations. In this chapter, we'll explore the key elements of future-proofing an influencer marketing strategy, including anticipating trends, investing in influencer relationships, leveraging data-driven insights, and building a flexible content strategy.

Brands that take a proactive, forward-thinking approach to influencer marketing are better positioned to sustain impact, build trust, and foster loyalty over the long term. This chapter will provide actionable guidance on creating a sustainable influencer marketing strategy that's equipped to navigate the unpredictable landscape ahead.

Section 1: Understanding and Anticipating Future Trends

Staying ahead of emerging trends is critical to future-proofing an influencer marketing strategy. By continuously monitoring shifts in technology, platform preferences, and consumer behaviors, brands can adapt quickly and capitalize on new opportunities.

1. Monitoring Emerging Trends and Platforms

New social media platforms frequently gain popularity, with TikTok and Twitch being prime examples. Brands that are quick to adopt these platforms can tap into fresh, engaged audiences while they're still growing. Staying informed about upcoming platforms or features allows brands to experiment early, positioning themselves as innovative leaders in the space.

Brands should allocate resources to track trends, which may include hiring social media experts, using social listening tools, or following industry influencers. By experimenting with new platforms like Clubhouse (for audio-based content) or Pinterest's video pins, brands can assess which platforms best support their goals and resonate with their target audience.

2. Adapting to Changes in Consumer Behavior

Consumer behavior is constantly evolving, often influenced by cultural shifts, technological advancements, and social issues. To future-proof a strategy, brands must be attentive to these changes and be ready to adapt. For instance, the rise in awareness around mental health has led to increased demand for content on self-care, mindfulness, and wellness.

Brands can adapt by conducting regular consumer research, gathering insights from surveys, focus groups, and social media analytics. This data enables brands to understand shifting consumer values and priorities, allowing them to create influencer partnerships and content that align with current audience expectations.

3. Preparing for Platform Algorithm Changes

Platform algorithms are continuously evolving, influencing how content is distributed and seen by audiences. For example, Instagram's algorithm now prioritizes Reels and Stories, while TikTok's "For You" page uses a complex algorithm to push certain types of content. Brands should be prepared for these shifts by understanding the algorithmic preferences of each platform and optimizing their influencer content accordingly.

To stay ahead, brands can encourage influencers to create content that aligns with algorithmic preferences, such as video-heavy posts or frequent Stories. Additionally, brands should regularly review analytics to identify which content performs best on each platform, allowing them to tailor their approach for maximum reach and engagement.

Section 2: Building Long-Term Relationships with Influencers

Long-term influencer relationships provide stability, authenticity, and adaptability, making them a cornerstone of a future-proof strategy. By focusing on genuine, lasting partnerships, brands create a network of loyal brand advocates who can help navigate shifts in consumer expectations or platform changes.

1. Establishing Trust and Loyalty with Influencers

Building trust is essential for any long-term partnership. Influencers who feel genuinely valued and respected by the brand are more likely to stay committed over time. Brands should prioritize open communication, fair compensation, and creative freedom to foster a sense of loyalty and mutual respect.

For instance, a brand might offer influencers performance-based bonuses or exclusive access to new product launches, reinforcing their importance in the brand's ecosystem. Regularly celebrating influencers' contributions and showing appreciation strengthens the relationship, increasing the likelihood of a lasting partnership.

2. Collaborating on Product Development

Involving influencers in product development adds authenticity and helps ensure that the brand's offerings align with consumer preferences. Influencers can provide valuable insights into trends, features, and aesthetic choices that resonate with their audience. For instance, a beauty brand might collaborate with a makeup influencer to co-create a product line, leveraging the influencer's expertise and credibility.

These collaborations foster a sense of ownership and pride in the brand, as influencers feel they've contributed to its success. Additionally, products developed with influencers' input are often received more positively by consumers, as they align closely with audience expectations.

3. Co-Creating Content Over Time

Brands should view influencers as creative partners, collaborating on content creation rather than treating them solely as amplifiers. Co-creating content allows influencers to integrate the brand more naturally into their lifestyle, resulting in authentic, engaging stories. Additionally, content that evolves over time resonates with audiences who see the brand become an integrated part of the influencer's life.

For example, a fitness brand could work with an influencer to document a personal fitness journey over several months, creating a long-term narrative that showcases the product's impact. This approach not only reinforces authenticity but also builds anticipation and engagement as followers witness the influencer's journey.

Section 3: Leveraging Data and Analytics for Continuous Improvement

Data-driven decision-making enables brands to optimize influencer strategies, measure campaign effectiveness, and identify areas for improvement. By continuously analyzing performance metrics, brands can make informed adjustments to ensure their strategies remain impactful and aligned with their goals.

1. Establishing a Comprehensive Data Strategy

A future-proof influencer marketing strategy requires a robust data strategy, with clear processes for gathering, analyzing, and utilizing performance metrics. Brands should establish KPIs for each campaign and track both short-term and long-term metrics, such as engagement rates, conversions, and brand sentiment.

Investing in analytics tools, such as Sprout Social, Brandwatch, or Google Analytics, provides brands with the insights they need to evaluate campaign success. These tools allow brands to gather data on influencer performance, audience demographics, and engagement patterns, enabling them to optimize future campaigns.

2. Identifying Key Metrics for Long-Term Success

While engagement metrics like likes and shares are useful for measuring immediate impact, long-term success requires a focus on metrics that reflect audience loyalty and brand reputation. Metrics such as customer lifetime value (CLV), repeat purchase rate, and net promoter score (NPS) provide insight into the sustained impact of influencer campaigns.

For example, tracking repeat purchase rates among customers acquired through influencer campaigns can reveal whether these consumers are building long-term loyalty. By focusing on these deeper metrics, brands gain a more accurate picture of their influencer campaigns' long-term value.

3. Conducting Post-Campaign Analysis and Applying Insights

Post-campaign analysis is essential for identifying what worked and what didn't. Brands should conduct thorough reviews of each campaign, examining KPIs, audience feedback, and influencer performance. This analysis provides actionable insights that can inform future campaigns, allowing brands to refine their strategies and build on past successes.

For instance, if data reveals that video content generated higher engagement than static images, brands can prioritize video in future campaigns. By continuously learning from each campaign, brands create a cycle of improvement that strengthens their influencer marketing strategy over time.

Section 4: Creating a Flexible and Diverse Content Strategy

To remain relevant, brands must develop a content strategy that's flexible enough to adapt to changing trends, platform updates, and audience preferences. A diverse content strategy allows brands to engage audiences through multiple formats, keeping campaigns fresh and engaging.

1. Experimenting with Various Content Formats

Different content formats appeal to different audiences, and experimenting with a variety of formats ensures brands can reach and resonate with a broader audience. By creating a mix of videos, Stories, Reels, blog posts, and live content, brands maintain a dynamic presence that adapts to evolving trends.

For example, a travel brand might produce destination guides through blog posts, capture immersive travel experiences through Instagram Reels, and host Q&A sessions with influencers on IG Live. This variety keeps followers engaged and helps the brand stay relevant across different platforms and content trends.

2. Encouraging Influencers to Showcase Creative Authenticity

To future-proof their content strategy, brands should encourage influencers to bring their unique perspectives and creativity to campaigns. By providing influencers with the flexibility to interpret the brand message in their own way, brands can produce content that feels genuine and resonates deeply with the audience.

For instance, instead of prescribing exact captions or visuals, a fashion brand might encourage influencers to style their pieces in a way that reflects their personal style, resulting in authentic content that feels true to the influencer's aesthetic.

3. Adapting to Platform-Specific Content Preferences

Each social media platform has its unique content preferences, and a future-proof content strategy should be tailored accordingly. For instance, Instagram favors visually appealing, curated images and videos, while TikTok prioritizes short-form, engaging, and often humorous content. Brands that adapt their content for each platform's audience are more likely to achieve success.

By understanding the characteristics of each platform, brands can guide influencers to create content that's optimized for maximum reach and engagement. For example, a skincare brand might focus on educational posts on YouTube, quick tips on TikTok, and beautiful product imagery on Instagram.

Section 5: Building a Strong Compliance and Ethical Framework

As influencer marketing grows, so does the importance of ethical practices and regulatory compliance. A future-proof strategy prioritizes transparency, aligns with evolving regulations, and incorporates ethical considerations to maintain trust with both influencers and audiences.

1. Establishing Ethical Guidelines for Influencer Partnerships

An ethical framework ensures that influencer partnerships reflect the brand's values, fostering trust and credibility. Brands should establish clear guidelines on issues such as responsible product representation, honesty in endorsements, and the types of influencers they will or will not work with.

For example, a wellness brand might establish guidelines that prioritize transparency around health claims, ensuring that influencers do not make exaggerated or false statements. These ethical guidelines protect both the brand and the influencer's credibility.

2. Staying Updated on Regulatory Changes

Regulations surrounding influencer marketing are constantly evolving, with increased scrutiny on transparency and disclosure. To avoid legal challenges and maintain trust, brands must stay informed of regulatory changes in each region they operate. This includes complying with disclosure requirements, data privacy laws, and advertising standards.

For instance, the FTC in the United States requires influencers to disclose partnerships clearly, while GDPR in the EU regulates data privacy practices. By establishing compliance protocols, brands can ensure that all campaigns meet legal requirements, protecting their reputation and consumer trust.

3. Conducting Regular Compliance Audits

To maintain ethical standards and ensure compliance, brands should conduct regular audits of their influencer marketing practices. These audits evaluate whether influencer content aligns with disclosure guidelines, brand safety protocols, and ethical standards. Compliance audits also provide an opportunity to review influencer contracts, ensuring they reflect current regulations and best practices.

By conducting these audits, brands demonstrate a commitment to ethical practices, building trust with both influencers and audiences and setting a foundation for sustainable, long-term success.

Conclusion: Building a Future-Proof Influencer Marketing Strategy

Creating a future-proof influencer marketing strategy is an ongoing process that requires adaptability, ethical commitment, and a focus on authentic connections. By anticipating trends, investing in long-term relationships, leveraging data insights, building a flexible content strategy, and adhering to ethical guidelines, brands can position themselves to thrive in an evolving landscape.

The future of influencer marketing will continue to be shaped by technological advancements, regulatory changes, and shifts in consumer behavior. Brands that embrace these changes and continuously refine their strategies are better positioned to sustain impact, foster loyalty, and build a strong, resilient presence in the influencer space.

As brands look forward, the goal should be not only to reach audiences but to build genuine, lasting connections that inspire trust, foster loyalty, and create meaningful impact. By preparing today, brands can set the foundation for an influencer marketing strategy that's equipped to endure, adapt, and succeed in the years to come.

Chapter 12: Evaluating and Optimizing Your Influencer Marketing Strategy

Introduction

Evaluating and optimizing your influencer marketing strategy is essential to ensuring that it continues to deliver value, remains aligned with brand goals, and adapts to shifting trends. While creating and launching influencer campaigns is a significant part of the process, ongoing evaluation allows brands to measure success, identify areas for improvement, and refine their strategies for future campaigns. This chapter will explore effective methods for evaluating influencer marketing campaigns, optimizing strategies based on insights, and implementing best practices to maximize ROI.

By systematically reviewing campaign performance, analyzing metrics, gathering feedback, and making data-driven adjustments, brands can ensure that their influencer marketing efforts are continually improving and delivering sustainable impact.

Section 1: Setting the Foundation for Evaluation

Effective evaluation starts with a well-defined framework that establishes goals, KPIs, and timelines. By defining what success looks like and determining the metrics that will be tracked, brands can conduct meaningful evaluations that reveal actionable insights.

1. Defining Clear Objectives and KPIs

The foundation of any evaluation process is a clear understanding of campaign objectives and key performance indicators (KPIs). Objectives might include raising brand awareness, increasing website traffic, generating leads, or driving conversions. KPIs, on the other hand, are specific metrics used to measure progress toward these goals. For example:

- **Awareness**: Reach, impressions, share of voice
- **Engagement**: Likes, comments, shares, engagement rate
- **Conversions**: Click-through rate (CTR), conversion rate, sales, customer acquisition cost
- **Loyalty**: Repeat purchase rate, customer lifetime value (CLV), brand sentiment

By defining these objectives and KPIs upfront, brands can evaluate campaigns more effectively, knowing which metrics to prioritize and which outcomes indicate success.

2. Establishing a Timeline for Measurement

Establishing a timeline for evaluation helps ensure that brands can track both immediate and long-term impact. While short-term metrics provide quick feedback on campaign performance, long-term metrics reveal lasting influence on brand loyalty and customer retention. For example:

- **Short-term**: Weekly or monthly reviews to monitor reach, engagement, and conversions.
- **Mid-term**: Quarterly reviews to analyze sustained engagement, brand sentiment, and repeat purchase rates.
- **Long-term**: Annual reviews to assess customer lifetime value, brand loyalty, and overall ROI.

This timeline allows brands to capture a comprehensive view of how each influencer campaign performs over time and adjust their approach accordingly.

3. Setting Up Benchmark Metrics for Comparison

To accurately assess campaign performance, brands need benchmark metrics that serve as a reference point. Benchmarks could include past campaign results, industry averages, or performance data from competitors. For example, if industry data shows an average engagement rate of 5% for influencer campaigns in a specific category, brands can compare their results against this benchmark to evaluate relative success.

Benchmarking provides context for performance metrics, helping brands understand whether their campaigns are meeting, exceeding, or falling short of expectations.

Section 2: Measuring Engagement, Reach, and Audience Sentiment

Engagement, reach, and audience sentiment are core metrics for evaluating how well an influencer campaign resonates with audiences. These indicators help brands gauge not only the reach of their message but also the quality of the connection it creates with the audience.

1. Evaluating Engagement Quality

While engagement rate is a key metric, the quality of engagement matters just as much as the quantity. High-quality engagement includes meaningful comments, questions, and interactions that demonstrate genuine interest in the brand. Metrics to evaluate engagement quality include:

- **Comment Depth**: Are followers leaving thoughtful comments or just quick emojis?

- **Question Rate**: Are followers asking questions about the product or seeking more information?
- **Share Rate**: How often is the content being shared by followers, indicating that it resonates deeply?

Evaluating engagement quality reveals whether the content is connecting authentically with followers, rather than simply attracting superficial interactions.

2. Analyzing Audience Reach and Impressions

Reach and impressions indicate the number of people who viewed the content, providing insight into brand visibility. Reach represents the unique number of individuals exposed to the content, while impressions indicate the total number of views, including repeat views by the same users. High reach and impression numbers can help boost brand recognition, making the brand more memorable to the audience.

Brands should analyze these metrics across different platforms to determine where their content is most effective. For instance, a campaign that performs exceptionally well on Instagram but receives less traction on TikTok might suggest a stronger alignment with the Instagram audience.

3. Conducting Sentiment Analysis

Sentiment analysis evaluates the tone of audience responses, determining whether comments and interactions are positive, neutral, or negative. Tools like Brandwatch, Sprout Social, and Hootsuite Insights offer sentiment analysis features that can track brand sentiment across influencer content.

A campaign that generates positive sentiment indicates that the audience feels favorably toward the brand, which can enhance brand loyalty and reputation. Conversely, negative sentiment may signal issues with the messaging or alignment with the influencer, providing an opportunity to address these concerns.

Section 3: Tracking Conversions and Sales

While engagement and reach are valuable indicators of awareness and interest, conversions and sales metrics reveal whether the campaign is driving tangible results. By tracking conversion rates, sales, and ROI, brands can determine the financial impact of their influencer partnerships.

1. Measuring Click-Through Rate (CTR) and Conversion Rate

Click-through rate (CTR) measures the percentage of users who clicked on a link or call-to-action in the influencer's content, while conversion rate indicates the percentage of those clicks that led to the desired action, such as a purchase or sign-up. These metrics are essential for campaigns focused on driving traffic and generating leads.

For example, a CTR of 2% and a conversion rate of 10% on an influencer's post promoting a limited-time offer provide insight into both interest and effectiveness. High CTR and conversion rates suggest strong interest and a compelling call-to-action, while low rates may indicate the need to refine messaging or targeting.

2. Calculating Cost Per Acquisition (CPA) and Return on Investment (ROI)

Cost per acquisition (CPA) and ROI are essential metrics for evaluating the cost-effectiveness of influencer campaigns. CPA measures the average cost to acquire a new customer through the campaign, while ROI calculates the overall profitability. By comparing these metrics to internal targets, brands can assess the campaign's financial performance.

Calculating CPA:

CPA   Total Campaign Cost   divided   by Number of Conversion

Calculating ROI:

ROI = Revenue from Campaign minus Total Campaign divided by Total Campaign Cost × 100

For instance, if a campaign cost $5,000 and generated $10,000 in revenue, the ROI would be:

ROI = 10,000 minus 5,000 divided by 5,000 multiplied by 100 = 100\%

A positive ROI indicates a profitable campaign, while a negative ROI suggests the need for optimization.

3. Tracking Customer Lifetime Value (CLV) for Long-Term Impact

Customer lifetime value (CLV) measures the total revenue generated by customers acquired through an influencer campaign over time. CLV provides insight into the campaign's long-term impact, showing whether the campaign attracts loyal customers who make repeat purchases.

For instance, if a new customer acquired through an influencer campaign has a CLV of $500, the brand can assess whether the campaign's cost was justified. High CLV rates indicate that influencer campaigns are effective in driving long-term brand loyalty and revenue.

Section 4: Gathering Qualitative Feedback from Influencers and Audiences

Quantitative metrics only tell part of the story. Qualitative feedback from influencers and audiences provides valuable insights into the campaign's strengths and areas for improvement, revealing opportunities for optimization.

1. Conducting Post-Campaign Reviews with Influencers

After each campaign, brands should hold post-campaign reviews with influencers to gather feedback. Influencers can provide insights into what resonated with their audience, any challenges they faced, and their suggestions for future campaigns. Questions for influencers might include:

- What type of content performed best with your audience?
- Did you encounter any difficulties while promoting the product?
- How could we improve our collaboration for future campaigns?

This feedback helps brands understand the influencer's experience and gain insights into what worked well, providing a basis for future improvements.

2. Collecting Audience Feedback through Surveys and Social Listening

Audience feedback is invaluable for evaluating campaign impact and identifying areas for improvement. Brands can gather feedback through surveys, comment analysis, and social listening tools to understand how followers perceive the brand and the influencer collaboration.

For example, a post-campaign survey could ask followers if they found the content informative, if they feel more positively about the brand, or if they're interested in purchasing the product. This feedback reveals how well the campaign met audience needs and expectations, highlighting areas to refine for future efforts.

3. Analyzing Customer Reviews and Sentiment on Social Media

Customer reviews and social media comments provide additional insight into the campaign's effectiveness and how the brand is perceived post-campaign. By analyzing reviews, brands can determine if the influencer campaign generated positive customer experiences or if there are areas for improvement in product quality or customer service.

For instance, a skincare brand may notice an increase in positive reviews after an influencer campaign, indicating that the product met or exceeded customer expectations. Conversely, if customers express dissatisfaction, the brand can take corrective action to address any issues.

Section 5: Applying Insights to Optimize Future Campaigns

Evaluation is only valuable if the insights are applied to future campaigns. By using data and feedback to optimize strategy, brands can improve campaign effectiveness, maximize ROI, and build stronger relationships with influencers and audiences.

1. Identifying Trends and Patterns in Performance

Brands should look for trends and patterns in past campaigns to understand what consistently drives success. For example, if video content consistently outperforms static images, or if certain influencers generate higher conversion rates, brands can prioritize these elements in future campaigns.

Recognizing these patterns allows brands to make data-driven decisions that enhance the impact of their influencer marketing efforts, maximizing effectiveness across all campaigns.

2. Testing New Strategies and Experimenting with Content

A/B testing and experimentation help brands refine their strategies and discover new ways to connect with audiences. Brands can test different messaging, visuals, content formats, and even influencer types to see what drives the highest engagement and conversions.

For example, a fashion brand might experiment with using micro-influencers in one campaign and macro-influencers in another, comparing performance to determine the best approach for their target audience.

3. Adjusting Influencer Selection Based on Performance Data

Evaluating influencer performance allows brands to refine their influencer selection process. Influencers who consistently drive high engagement, conversions, and positive sentiment may be ideal candidates for long-term partnerships. Conversely, influencers who underperform may not be the best fit for future campaigns.

By selecting influencers based on performance data, brands can optimize partnerships, building a network of trusted influencers who consistently deliver results.

4. Implementing a Cycle of Continuous Improvement

Optimizing influencer marketing is an ongoing process. By establishing a cycle of continuous improvement—where each campaign is evaluated, insights are applied, and strategies are refined—brands can create a self-sustaining system that continually improves performance and maximizes ROI.

Conclusion: Cultivating a Culture of Evaluation and Optimization

Evaluating and optimizing an influencer marketing strategy requires a commitment to learning, growth, and adaptability. By setting clear objectives, gathering quantitative and qualitative feedback, and applying insights to improve future campaigns, brands can ensure that their influencer marketing efforts remain effective, relevant, and aligned with their long-term goals.

A culture of evaluation and optimization empowers brands to navigate changes, adapt to evolving audience preferences, and build stronger relationships with influencers. This approach not only maximizes ROI but also establishes a sustainable influencer marketing strategy that's equipped to deliver lasting impact in an ever-changing digital landscape. By embracing a mindset of continuous improvement, brands can build a foundation for success in influencer marketing that endures well into the future.

Conclusion: The Power of Authentic Influence

Influencer marketing has transformed the way brands connect with audiences, offering a powerful avenue for building trust, fostering loyalty, and driving impactful engagement. But as the industry has evolved, so too has the importance of authenticity—a quality that has emerged as the cornerstone of effective influencer partnerships. Authentic influence is no longer about one-off promotions or quick sales; it's about creating lasting, genuine connections that resonate on a personal level and build meaningful relationships with consumers.

At its core, authentic influence goes beyond likes and shares. It's rooted in mutual respect, shared values, and a commitment to transparency. For brands, embracing authenticity means selecting influencers whose values align with their mission, giving them creative freedom, and focusing on building trust rather than pushing sales. Authenticity requires that brands recognize influencers as more than just marketing tools; they are storytellers, advocates, and partners who have the unique ability to humanize a brand and make it relatable to audiences.

This book has explored the elements of building authentic partnerships—from defining brand values and identifying the right influencers to crafting compelling, value-driven content and measuring success in ways that go beyond superficial metrics. In an age where audiences are more skeptical than ever, authentic influence is what sets brands apart, creating a space where trust can thrive and messages can have a lasting impact.

The future of influencer marketing lies in relationships that are built to endure. Brands that invest in long-term partnerships, prioritize genuine engagement, and embrace a culture of continuous improvement are better positioned to navigate the evolving landscape and create lasting value. As new platforms emerge, trends shift, and consumer expectations change, the brands that remain adaptable, transparent, and committed to authenticity will be the ones that succeed.

In a world full of fleeting digital interactions, authentic influence cuts through the noise, fostering connections that feel real, honest, and valuable. It is this power of authentic influence that allows brands to inspire, connect, and ultimately, make a difference in the lives of their audiences. As you move forward, remember that the heart of successful influencer marketing isn't just the reach or the metrics—it's the impact your brand has on people's lives, the stories you tell together, and the trust you build along the way.

Appendices: Essential Resources, Tools, and Communities for Influencer Marketing Success

To maximize the impact of your influencer marketing efforts, having the right resources, tools, and support communities at your fingertips is invaluable. Below is a curated list of essential platforms, analytics tools, educational resources, and online communities to help you navigate the influencer marketing landscape more effectively.

---

1. Influencer Discovery & Management Platforms

These platforms help brands find, connect with, and manage influencers based on key metrics like engagement rate, audience demographics, and content focus.

- **Upfluence**: Allows brands to search for influencers based on keywords, audience data, and engagement. Offers campaign tracking and CRM features.
- **AspireIQ**: A full-service influencer marketing platform that helps brands find influencers, manage relationships, and track campaign performance.

- **Traackr**: Provides robust tools for influencer discovery, campaign management, and performance analysis.
- **Influencity**: Offers an extensive database for finding influencers, with detailed analytics on audience quality and campaign tracking tools.
- **HYPR**: Focuses on audience insights, allowing brands to find influencers based on detailed demographic and psychographic information.

2. Social Media Analytics & Listening Tools

Analyzing audience sentiment, engagement, and reach is critical for measuring the success of influencer campaigns. These tools provide insights into how your brand is perceived and help track campaign performance across platforms.

- **Sprout Social**: A comprehensive social media management tool with detailed analytics, social listening, and reporting features.
- **Brandwatch**: Advanced social listening and sentiment analysis tool that allows brands to monitor conversations and trends across social media.
- **Hootsuite Insights**: Offers social listening and analytics to track brand sentiment,

audience engagement, and influencer performance.

- **BuzzSumo**: Helps track trending content, discover influencers, and monitor social engagement around specific keywords or topics.
- **Talkwalker**: Combines social listening and analytics, providing insights into brand sentiment, trending topics, and influencer reach.

3. Campaign Tracking & Performance Analysis

To assess the ROI of influencer campaigns, these tools provide insights into clicks, conversions, and customer behavior.

- **Google Analytics**: Tracks traffic and conversions from influencer campaigns, helping brands understand how influencers drive engagement on their website.
- **Bitly**: A link-shortening and tracking tool that provides detailed click data for each link, useful for tracking influencer campaign performance.
- **Refersion**: A platform for tracking affiliate links and influencer conversions, ideal for campaigns involving commissions or performance-based compensation.

- **Impact**: Manages partnerships and tracks influencer-driven sales with analytics for conversions, ROI, and CLV.
- **Linktree**: Popular among influencers, this tool consolidates multiple links into one, providing analytics on click-through rates for each linked resource.

4. Content Creation & Collaboration Tools

These tools support collaboration with influencers, allowing brands to co-create content and manage the creative process effectively.

- **Canva**: An easy-to-use graphic design tool that enables influencers to create professional-quality visuals for campaigns.
- **Asana**: A project management tool that helps organize tasks, track deadlines, and manage campaign workflows collaboratively.
- **Dropbox**: Provides a cloud-based storage solution for sharing content assets, such as images, videos, and brand guidelines.
- **Trello**: A visual project management tool that allows brands and influencers to organize and track content creation.
- **Google Workspace**: A suite of tools including Google Docs, Sheets, and Drive, ideal for sharing briefs, tracking budgets, and collaborating in real time.

5. Educational Resources & Courses

For brands and marketers looking to deepen their understanding of influencer marketing strategies, these resources offer courses, certifications, and insights.

- **HubSpot Academy: Influencer Marketing Strategy**: A free course covering the basics of influencer marketing, including influencer selection, content planning, and campaign measurement.
- **Hootsuite Academy: Social Media Marketing Certification**: Provides a broad overview of social media marketing, including influencer marketing strategies.
- **Digital Marketing Institute**: Offers comprehensive courses on digital marketing, with modules focused on influencer marketing, content strategy, and social media analytics.
- **Influencer Marketing Hub**: A free resource with guides, articles, and templates on influencer marketing topics, including platform comparisons and industry news.
- **Coursera (Various Institutions)**: Courses from top universities on social media marketing, content creation, and analytics, many of which include influencer marketing components.

6. Communities & Networking Groups

Connecting with other marketers, influencers, and industry professionals is invaluable for staying current with trends, exchanging ideas, and finding collaboration opportunities.

- **Facebook Groups (e.g., Influencer Marketing Hub Community)**: A place for marketers, brands, and influencers to share tips, ask questions, and discuss trends in influencer marketing.
- **Reddit (e.g., r/InfluencerMarketing)**: An active forum where members share news, strategies, and challenges related to influencer marketing.
- **LinkedIn Groups (e.g., Influencer Marketing Professionals)**: Connects marketers, agencies, and brands, offering a space to discuss challenges, share resources, and network with peers.
- **Clubhouse Rooms (Social Media Marketing and Influencer Marketing)**: Provides live discussions with industry experts on topics like influencer strategy, brand partnerships, and platform trends.
- **MarketingProfs PRO Community**: A subscription-based community offering access to webinars, reports, and networking with industry experts in influencer and digital marketing.

7. Legal & Compliance Resources

Navigating the legal and ethical aspects of influencer marketing is crucial. These resources provide guidance on compliance with advertising regulations and data privacy.

- **FTC Guidelines on Influencer Marketing**: Detailed guidelines from the Federal Trade Commission on advertising disclosures and compliance for influencer marketing in the U.S.
- **ASA (UK) Influencer Guidelines**: The UK's Advertising Standards Authority offers guidelines for brands and influencers to comply with advertising transparency requirements.
- **GDPR Compliance (EU)**: Resources from the European Union that help brands understand data protection regulations, especially important for brands collecting audience data.
- **Influencer Marketing Hub's Disclosure Checklist**: A practical checklist for ensuring compliance with influencer marketing disclosure requirements.
- **ClearCode**: A resource that provides information on ethical practices in influencer marketing, including brand safety and transparency recommendations.

Final Thoughts

Equipped with these resources, tools, and community connections, brands can navigate the multifaceted world of influencer marketing with greater ease and confidence. By combining the right technology with continuous learning and a supportive network, marketers can build a strategy that not only achieves measurable results but also remains adaptable and aligned with industry best practices.

Authentic, impactful influencer marketing requires more than creativity and strategy; it requires the support of a well-rounded toolkit and a commitment to ongoing learning. With these resources at your fingertips, you're well on your way to building lasting, effective, and ethical partnerships that deliver real value for your brand and its audiences.